Forum on Arab and Muslim Affairs
FAMA Conference Volume

NGOs in the Arab World Post-Arab Uprisings: Domestic and International Politics of Funding and Regulation

Conference Series
Summer 2016

TADWEEN PUBLISHING

NGOs in the Arab World Post-Arab Uprisings: Domestic and International Politics of Funding and Regulation

Majid Al Muthhaji
Wahid Farchichi
Menna Omar
Firas Jaber & Iyad Al Riyahi

Project Directors: Noura Erakat & Nizar Saghieh

With Introduction by Noura Erakat

Translated from Arabic by Mazen Hakeem,
Aiman Haddad, and Tania Georgi

 **THE LEGAL AGENDA**

This research project and workshop is co-sponsored by the Arab Studies Institute, The Legal Agenda, and The Asfari Institute for Civil Society and Citizenship.

Printed in the United States of America
First Printing: August 2016
ISBN: 978-1-939067-22-7

This publication is produced in part with the support of the Middle East Program at George Mason University, with which the Arab Studies Institute is affiliated.

Acknowledgements

This study could not have been completed without the leadership of Nizar Saghieh, a Lebanese human rights attorney and co-founder of the Legal Agenda. Saghieh's well-established record in the Arab world provided the research initiative with instant credibility among, and access to, the researchers we recruited. We are also grateful to the Asfari Institute, and particularly Fateh Azzam and Rania Masri, as well as Fawwaz Tarabulsi and Ziad Abdel Samad for participating in the research workshop and providing the researchers with incisive feedback. Thanks also to the diligent and unseen labor that made the research workshop possible, in particular Elie Haddad on behalf of the Arab Studies Institute as well as the Asfari Institute for Civil Society and Citizenship. This manuscript could not be completed without the support of Tadween Publishing's excellent translators, copy editors, and managing editors, namely Jen Curatola, Katie Jackson, Alicia Cagle, and John Warner. Special gratitude is owed to Bassam Haddad, who on behalf of the Arab Studies Institute, insisted that we initiate a critical study related to human rights in the Arab world following the Uprisings and who participated in nearly every step of the process from finding researchers, organizing the workshop, and publishing the manuscript. Finally, the greatest thanks is owed to the researchers themselves overcame significant obstacles and endured personal risk in their tremendous efforts to help produce incredibly textured and much-needed knowledge on civil society trends in the Arab world in the aftermath of the Arab uprisings, namely Menna Omar, Majid Al Muthhaji, Wahid Farchichi, Firas Jaber, and Iyad Al Riyahi.

Noura Erakat
Summer 2016

Table of Contents

Introduction
Noura Erakat

Purpose of Study

The Arab uprisings that began in December 2011 in Tunisia have created a series of ongoing processes throughout the Arab world. Massive popular movements led to the removal of long-standing autocrats in Tunisia, Egypt, and Yemen. International intervention and an armed rebel movement also led to the removal of Libya's head of state. Today, the uprisings in Bahrain, Yemen, and Syria have become consumed by civil war driven by proxy regional interests. While revolutions, and counterrevolutions, continue in nearly all of these countries, until late 2011 they were sites of unfettered optimism and euphoria.

Whatever could be said about the varied meanings of these movements, Arab populations have successfully asserted themselves as active subjects constitutive of the state rather than its indistinguishable and expendable objects. In this context, civil society within the Arab world became very "sexy" among scholars, donors, and governments alike. This piqued interest generated new funding opportunities, new exchanges of expertise, new studies, and hundreds of conferences all eager to explore and explain what had happened, what was happening, and what was going to happen next.

The creation of new organizations, non-profit corporations, and non-governmental organizations, were among the primary consequences of such international interest. Despite their salient role, the precise status of these organizations (i.e., number, origins, funding sources), and their implications has received little scrutiny. The dearth of such research has left a gaping hole in the analysis of transformative social change and ongoing conflict throughout the region.

This research initiative seeks to contribute to this scarce literature in four contexts: Egypt, Tunisia, Yemen, and Palestine. While foreign funding led to the creation of new opportunities for otherwise marginalized communities in Tunisia, in Egypt new regimes targeted non-governmental organizations (NGOs) as sources of national discord and instability. Meanwhile, in Palestine, where NGOs have proliferated since the early nineties, professional activism has supplanted popular mobilization and helped to contain, rather than resolve, the conflict. In Yemen, the uprisings marked a regression for NGO development and intensified sectarian divisions between them. The aim of this research initiative is to explore these dynamics more thoroughly.

The research findings are not exhaustive and can be further developed. Their purpose is to provide an empirical basis upon which to develop research. They can also be the first pieces in a region-wide research initiative that includes other sites of significant or incremental change including Libya, Morocco, Jordan, Bahrain, and Kuwait. In addition to expanding the scope of these findings, the research initiative can also benefit from greater depth. In particular, a thorough literature review on civil society organizations stands to significantly enrich this *Conference Series*.

RESEARCH METHODOLOGY

The Legal Agenda and Arab Studies Institute in collaboration with the Asfari Institute vetted and chose one to two researchers in Egypt, Yemen, Tunisia, and Palestine to conduct research. They asked researchers to consider the following questions as they laid out their research agenda:

1. How many NGOs have been established since the aftermath of the Arab uprisings? (If organizations have been formed as corporations or law firms due to domestic law, include those and indicate the relevant restrictions)
2. What was the total number of NGOs before the uprisings? What is the total number as of January 2014?
3. What foundations are the primary funders of NGOs in your country of interest? Are there any pervasive conditions that they impose upon all recipients?
4. Has the staff of particular NGOs significantly increased? If so, which ones and how have they grown?
5. What is the relationship between NGOs and political parties, if any?
6. What is the average staff size of NGOs? Indicate the staff size for the most relevant NGOs.
7. What is the primary output of existing and new NGOs i.e., reports, press releases, policy recommendations?
8. What is the primary activity of existing and new NGOs i.e., direct services, international advocacy, domestic lobbying, strategic litigation, public awareness, media campaigns?
9. What is the role of international law and human rights in the mission of each NGO?
10. Does the NGO have unique relationships to foreign states? If so, to which ones and what does that relationship look like?
11. What laws govern the regulation and activities of existing and new NGOs?

Beyond the provision of guiding questions, the sponsoring institutions did not impose a single methodological approach upon the researchers. That, together with the distinct contexts of each country, or country under occupation in the case of Palestine, resulted in starkly divergent findings.

Researchers in Tunisia and Palestine used a similar approach: a quantitative overview of NGO development based upon data from the Ministry of Interior that reveals the geographic distribution of the NGOs as well as their annual growth. The researchers then conducted interviews with, and distributed a questionnaire to, a sample of the listed NGOs. Researchers in Palestine and Tunisia buttressed their findings with existing literature and available news sources. Whereas Yemen, Tunisia, and Egypt experienced uprisings and a transition, in Palestine there is no state and there were no uprisings. The researchers therefore chose 2006 as the critical juncture to examine since that was the year in which Hamas won parliamentary elections. Their sample included forty-two NGOs distributed between the West Bank and the Gaza Strip. In Tunisia, the researchers conducted 120 interviews (one-on-one, phone, and in three working groups) and received fifty-five responses to their questionnaire. They chose January 2011 as the pivotal juncture in their research because that was the month of Zine Al Abidine Ben Ali's departure.

Due to a hostile environment in Egypt, the researcher could not obtain data from the Ministry of Solidarity and had to estimate the total number of NGOs based upon existing literature. The researcher narrowed the sample pool to human rights NGOs in particular. Those NGOs receive international funding, are targeted by the government, and have been visible in the transitional process. The researcher then narrowed the sample size to twelve human rights NGOs based on their level of activity. She sent them a questionnaire and conducted interviews with them. The researcher buttressed her findings with existing literature and news media. She chose February 2011 as the pivotal juncture marking the departure of Hosni Mubarak, as well as July 2013 marking the military coup led by Abdel Fattah Al Sisi. Only one of the twelve human rights NGOs examined was established after 2011.

The Yemen researcher examined developments among NGOs between 2011 and 2014. Due to the ongoing conflict in Yemen, the researcher did not conduct interviews or distribute questionnaires. Instead, the research is based on data from the Ministry of Social Affairs and Labor and coupled with existing literature and news media.

Upon completion of their first drafts, researchers, together with discussants from the sponsoring institutions, convened a workshop in Beirut, Lebanon in October 2014 to discuss their initial findings. Following this workshop, the participating discussants submitted feedback to each of the researchers and asked for revisions and clarification. The researchers submitted their revised findings in July 2015.

SUMMARY OF FINDINGS

Ongoing turmoil hampered research in each of the four contexts. Palestine witnessed yet another devastating military offensive against the besieged Gaza Strip in the summer of 2014. Egypt witnessed a terse presidential reign by the

Muslim Brotherhood that culminated in a military coup in July 2013 and a counterrevolution that persists. What was once hailed as a bloodless transition in Yemen has devolved into a bloody civil war marked by sectarianism and maintained by proxy regional forces. Tunisia has fared relatively better than its aforementioned counterparts. However, even it has not been spared from an ongoing, and often violent, struggle to assume power and the monopoly over the use of force. Notwithstanding these challenges, the researchers completed a herculean task in documenting new hurdles facing NGOs, new opportunities that have become available to them, and confrontations with both their society and state. Due to these challenges, as well as divergent methodological approaches, there is little to moderate resonance among the research findings.

DISTINCT CONTEXTS

The lack of more significant resonance among the reports reflects their distinct contexts. Palestine has no state and is, therefore, unique for boasting a civil society without a state. Additionally, Palestine has not experienced an Arab uprising. Nevertheless, it has been the site of a significantly large number of NGOs since the early nineties and similarly underwent a boon in its civil society sector. In order to properly study the impact of foreign intervention as well as local developments, the researchers chose to study the growth of NGOs following the 2006 electoral victory of Hamas. Following this juncture, international donors flocked to support a particular political agenda. Rather than support civil society generally, international donors supported Fatah-affiliated organizations. In order to avoid the legal trappings associated with supporting Hamas, designated as a terrorist organization by the United States and the European Union, international NGOs established local chapters in the Gaza Strip rather than support Gaza-based Palestinian organizations. According to the Palestinian Ministry of Interior, individuals established 1,520 new NGOs between 2006 and 2014, at an average rate of 191 new organizations each year. This rate of growth is historically unparalleled. The number of new NGOs established in eight years is nearly double the total number of NGOs established between 1966 and 2005 (1,243 NGOs). Of the 1,520 organizations established since 2006, 83.5 percent were established in the West Bank, while 16.5 percent of them were established in the Gaza Strip.

Yemen is particularly distinct because unlike other contexts where the Arab uprisings marked a surge in civil society organizations, the uprising in Yemen marked a slight regression. The end of Yemen's division in 1990 marked the first significant juncture in the history of its civil society. Upon the unification of the war-torn country in the early nineties, Yemenis began to organize themselves in NGOs. However, the concept of NGOs paled alongside other formations, namely tribe/clan formations. Nonetheless, civil society organizations steadily grew and experienced a boon between 2001 and 2011. By late 2011, registered NGOs numbered 8,371. Between the ouster of Ali Abdullah Saleh in 2011 and 2013, individuals established 1,383 new organizations bringing the total number of NGOs to 9,700. The ouster of Saleh in 2011 initiated a transitional phase that has since devolved into a civil war. Since his departure, civil society organizations have taken on a sectarian dimension and become more starkly affiliated with national political trends rather than a distinct grassroots counter-culture.

Tunisia is unique for being the first country to successfully remove an autocratic ruler. The promise that Tunisia offered to the rest of the Middle East helps to explain the significant boon in civil society organizations following Ben Ali's removal from power. Individuals established 10,000 organizations in thirty-three years between 1988 and 2011. Between 2011 and 2013, following Ben Ali's ouster, they established approximately 7,245 new organizations, at a rate of approximately 2,000 new associations each year. This spike in the number of NGOs is partly explained by legislative amendments. The transitional leadership amended the law governing NGOs making it easier to establish a new organization and reducing governmental oversight. Prior to 2014, the Tunisian regime strictly controlled civil society and leveraged it to "polish" its image among the international community. Most NGOs established after the first political shift in Tunisia in November 1987 sought to improve elementary education and lacked a political agenda. In contrast, the boon since Ben Ali's ouster in 2014 is marked by "spontaneity, independence, and struggle." The spike in NGOs is also explained by international donor enthusiasm. For example, the European Union and the United Nations Development Fund contributed 24 million Tunisian dinars to civil society organizations between 2011 and 2014.

Egypt is the largest Arab state and is the site of the greatest number of NGOs by far. Though exact numbers are unavailable, an estimated 24,600 NGOs existed as of 2010. At first, the removal of Hosni Mubarak signaled a boon in NGOs as international funding spiked and kept pace with national enthusiasm to steward a post-revolutionary Egypt. That positive trend reversed after the military coup in July 2013. At this juncture, NGOs joined the criticism of the regime for its excessive use of force and its detention policies toward protestors. In response, the state "launched a war against these organizations." State forces stormed NGO offices, confiscated their equipment, and interrogated their employees. The Ministry of Social Consolidation also drafted a law aimed at truncating the number of NGOs as well as their permissible mandate. In response to a campaign mounted by a coalition of NGOs against the law, the Ministry decided to undergo a case-by-case review of each NGO instead; a move that nevertheless hovers as a constant threat to their activities and the safety of their employees.

Trends

Despite their distinct contexts and divergent methodological approaches, a few common trends appeared among the four case studies. These included an increase in international funding with political overtones; shifts in the relationship between civil society and the state on the one hand, and society on the other; and distinctions within the class of NGOs indicating broader societal shifts. These trends merit greater study and comparison.

INTERNATIONAL FUNDING

The boon of civil society organizations across Palestine, Yemen, Egypt, and Tunisia is attributable to international funding. Such funding has come with its biases reflective of governmental interests. In some instances, the flow of donor funding has a determinant impact. This is not always the case, as civil society in some contexts has collaborated to push back against donor demands or to refuse their funding altogether. Still in other contexts, governmental restrictions on the flow of international aid have tempered the impact of such intervention.

In Palestine, "the financial support is only given because the community of international donors is concerned with ensuring the continuity of certain 'functions,' which can support Palestinian society and always keeps it one step away from complete breakdown." For example, international donors heed Israel's military restrictions on the movement of goods and people. Rather than provide aid to challenge those restrictions, donors provide aid based on their conditional acceptance. In effect, while donor aid to NGOs can help alleviate the harsh conditions of Israel's occupation, it also reinforces and legitimizes Israel's infrastructure of control. Moreover, since Hamas's assumption of power in the Gaza Strip in 2007, foreign donors have joined in the boycott of Hamas. They have also halted their aid to "non-governmental Islamic projects and joint projects of Islamic and non-Islamic organizations."

In the immediate aftermath of Ben Ali's removal, international donors flocked to support new associations in Tunisia. Most of them funded hitherto prohibited activities, which were related to civil and political rights and categorized as "citizenship projects." These included not only traditional donors like the United Nations, the European Union, France, and Germany but also new funders including the Open Society Foundation, Holland, Denmark, the United Kingdom, Sweden, Finland, Switzerland, as well as donor organizations from the United States and Qatar. Support for associations increased by as much as four times for some organizations after 2011. Funding during this three-year period came in two stages: the first lasted until nearly eight months following national elections in October 2013. This funding lacked coordination and was not closely monitored. From mid-2012 to the present, donors have become more stringent in their provision of funds and have discerned organizations based on their strategy, funding sustainability, and demonstrated work product.

The most significant donors in Yemen include several US institutions like the Department of State, the National Endowment of Democracy, and the National Democratic Institute for International Affairs, and the US Agency for International Development. They also include several UN agencies, the German

Agency for International Cooperation, CARE of France, and Oxfam of Britain, among others. Following Ali Abdullah Saleh's removal, Saudi Arabia convened a donors' conference for Yemen's development in Riyadh. Donor pressure resulted in a commitment by Yemen's transitional government to strengthen its relationship with civil society organizations. The agreement stipulated that government would establish a higher council to oversee these relationships. Forty percent (40%) of the higher council would be government representatives while sixty percent (60%) would be representatives of civil society organizations. Priority would be given to the most vulnerable communities. Although the higher council should have been announced in June 2014, it has yet to be established. Reasons for the delay include anxiety by some organizations that politically-affiliated NGOs within the council will lead to a government takeover of the body by other means. Additionally, several new NGOs established after 2011 have been explicitly excluded. Despite the donor pressure to establish a higher council and prioritize civil society, it has not moved forward in Yemen.

Egypt-based NGOs are numerous and were well-established before the uprisings that began in early 2011. The human rights NGOs are dependent on international aid and all of the twelve organizations included in the study consider funding a partnership with the financier. Still, they have collaborated to resist donor prerogatives by submitting their grants for funding without consideration for significant amendment. Six of the organizations refuse funding from governments and their embassies as a matter of principle. Another two accept it on a case-by-case basis. In general, there is a greater level of trust in European funding agencies than in American ones. Following the removal of Mubarak in late January 2011, international funding helped NGOs expand their staff as well as their project areas. The uprisings also witnessed the growth of youth initiatives that refused to organize themselves as NGOs but instead maintained the form of a loose network. These initiatives did not seek nor receive funding.

BATTLE AGAINST THE STATE & SOCIETAL DISTRUST

As a result of the internecine conflict between Fatah and Hamas, Palestinian NGOs across the political spectrum suffered. Both ruling parties in the West Bank and the Gaza Strip introduced new procedures for establishing NGOs including new bylaws standards, security checks, tax clearance, and bank account clearances. These legal hurdles enabled ruling parties to make it more cumbersome to establish and/or maintain an NGO. It also allowed them to verify the political affiliation of the founding members of NGOs thus controlling their numbers. The MoI in the Gaza Strip shut down more than forty-two associations while the MoI in the West Bank shut down more than one hundred associations and centers.

The relationship between Tunisian society and civil society was especially tense before the 2011 transition and continues to influence the perception of associations. Until 2011, the regime had coopted civil society in order to improve its image before the international community. Moreover, Tunisian society has not valued civil society because its efficacy is not visibly tangible or quantifiable. Additionally, Tunisian society could not easily distinguish the work of associations and national and local political machinations. While societal support for civil society associations has not markedly improved, Tunisia's transitional government dramatically altered its relationship with them. In particular, the transitional government annulled the 1959 law regulating associations that enabled the state to control, penetrate, and monitor associations. The 2011 decree canceled this law and made it easier to establish and maintain independent organizations. The decree has made membership the purview of each association; reduced the age of eligibility to establish an association from twenty to sixteen; made residents, and not just citizens of Tunisia, able to establish associations; and subjected government regulation of associations to judicial oversight, among other advances. These positive developments set the Tunisian case study apart from the other country case studies in this *Conference Series*.

Following the removal of Yemen's Saleh in 2011, the government's security and political grip on civil society dramatically loosened. Whereas, prior to 2011, the Ministry of Social Affairs and Labor played a significant oversight function in the establishment of new associations marked by close scrutiny of well-known activists, since the transition there is less strict oversight. As a result of this shift, Saleh's removal in 2011 led to an immediate spike in NGOs that quickly waned. This trend led to a significant rise of NGOs related to Islamist movements, especially to the Political Islamist Movement represented by the Yemeni Gathering Platform for Reform. Even Saleh's General People's Congress Party began to organize themselves in NGOs in order to fill the political vacuum and to benefit from international funding. The political space also allowed long-time activists to form organizations as well like the Citizenship Organization for Human Rights. These organizations could not escape the sectarian polarization shaping Yemeni national politics, a process exacerbated by the National Dialogue process. These battles subsumed their organizational goals and ultimately led to a decline in their activities. Moreover, because these NGOs have been associated with well-known individuals and have functioned like mini authoritarian regimes, they are viewed with skepticism to disdain among Yemeni society.

The Egyptian regime "launched a war" against civil society following the military coup in early July. Notwithstanding their scrutiny of the Muslim Brotherhood during its presidential tenure, NGOs became a target once their scrutiny shifted onto the Sisi regime. In particular, NGOs criticized the regime's excessive use of force and liberal detention policies toward the Muslim Brotherhood. Regime forces raided the offices of the Egyptian Center for Economic and Social Rights twice between December 2013 and May 2014. In July 2014, the Ministry of Solidarity publicly threatened NGOs to register as civil associations, rather than non-profit civil and legal firms. NGOs that failed to register would be dissolved and/or their leading employees and board members would be legally prosecuted. In response, twenty-three human rights organizations submitted a memo objecting to the law and requested a dialogue. Civil society organizations also launched a campaign in October 2014 called *Civil Society is a Right for You and Me* in order to rehabilitate its tarnished image among Egyptian society. Ultimately, the ministry decided to review each organization on a case-by-case basis. Although the regime did not materialize its threats against NGOs, the organizations realize that the regime's ability to do so at any time is a real possibility.

CHARITIES, NGOS, AND OTHER INTERNAL DISTINCTIONS

In each of these contexts, NGOs work as a stand-in for a much broader category that represents societal associations independent of the government. There are several internal distinctions within the NGO categories that represent societal trends. Among these distinctions is one between charity associations and NGOs. Charity associations seek to provide basic services like health, education, and basic goods and tend to be religious in nature. In contrast, NGOs are generally secular and have a more pointed agenda dealing with political reform like human rights and the rule of law. This description is overly broad and glosses over the more intricate distinctions between various civil associations in each context but works to identify a salient trend among the case studies.

By 2005, charity associations (40.4 percent) constituted the largest number of associations in Palestine followed by youth and sports organizations (30.4 percent). Human rights organizations constituted 2.6 percent of all associations. Following Hamas's parliamentary victory in 2006 and preceding its jurisdictional control over the Gaza Strip in 2007, charities grew at a relatively slower rate than other associations. Between 2006 and 2014, individuals established 177 new charities; 235 new youth and sports associations; ninety-eight new human rights associations; and 197 new women's associations. Forty percent of all new organizations established during this time were established in Ramallah, the nominal capital of the West Bank.

This distinction assumes a geographic dimension in Tunisia. Of the 7,245 associations established between 2011 and 2014, 1,898 associations were established in the Greater Tunis area. Sixty-nine percent of those associations are human rights organizations. In contrast, only 810 of new associations were established in the southeast of the country. Nearly 25 percent of them are charity associations with religious dimensions. In total, since 2011, of all associations established, 1,200 are charity associations; 1,100 are cultural and artistic associations; 980 are developmental associations; two hundred are human rights organizations; and sixty-eight are women's rights organizations. Prior to the transition in Tunisia, the state categorized associations into three categories: normal (with eight sub-categories), national interest, and foreign associations.

The 2011 decree annulled these categories. Nearly 16 percent of the 120 organizations interviewed, distribute food and aid to communities in need. This indicates a more fluid distinction between NGOs and charities.

The distinction in Yemen is between cooperative unions and civil institutions. The former category includes general, sociable, consumer, intellectual, residential, sea related, and crafts. Civil institutions are comprised of charities; institutions; social, cultural, professional, and scientific institutions; and fraternities. By the end of 2013, individuals registered 1925 cooperative unions and 7,356 civil associations. Agricultural associations constituted the largest number of cooperative unions while social associations constituted the largest number of civil institutions. All organizations are disproportionately concentrated in San'aa and its provinces. While human rights organizations, trade unions, and developmental initiatives are similarly registered under one of these two categories, they are distinctly regarded as NGOs for having a political agenda.

In Egypt, NGOs take distinct legal forms depending on their mission. Civil associations are those NGOs regulated closely by the government. They include charities and are dependent on donations from Egyptians. They work to provide basic goods, education, health, and care for vulnerable communities. A few human rights organizations take this form as well. The vast majority of human rights NGOs register as non-profit law firms or non-profit civil firms in order to escape the excessive control of the government. Although the latest draft of the Egyptian constitution provides for the freedom of assembly (Article 73) and the freedom to form civil associations and institutions (Article 75), the NGO law allows for significant government intervention into the affairs of NGOs. This includes eliminating members of the NGO's administrative council deemed unsuitable without review. NGOs registered as non-profit law and civil firms receive funding from international donors, subjecting them to additional scrutiny.

CONCLUSION AND NEXT STEPS

These trends and observations are not comprehensive. The research findings feature other cleavages regarding NGO corruption, employment conditions, and societal shifts not described above in great detail. More significantly, perhaps, are the myriad divergences, in substance and methodological approach, which merit greater scrutiny. This summary of the findings is intended to provide a snapshot of some of the most salient trends among the four case studies: Egypt, Yemen, Tunisia, and Palestine. Next steps for building on this *Conference Series* include continuing the research across the region for greater comparative perspective both as case studies for the impact of the Arab uprisings as well as to examine the development of NGOs under relatively "calm" circumstances. In the case that this initiative is continued, an optimal methodological approach should be suggested to all researchers for the sake of greater internal coherence. In addition to producing new supplementary material, these findings are intended to provide an empirical basis upon which to develop research. Next steps also include developing a literature review of material on civil society organizations in general and in the Middle East in particular.

RESEARCHER BIOS

Majid Al Muthhaji is a Yemeni writer and researcher based in Yemen.

Wahid Farchichi is Professor of Law at the University of Tunis and president of the Tunisian Association for the Defense of Individual Freedoms.

Menna Omar is a staff researcher of international law, particularly humanitarian and human rights law at the Legal Agenda.

Firas Jaber & Iyad Al Riyahi are Palestine-based researchers with Al Marsad, a community initiative aimed at evaluating the intellectual, institutional, and colonialist frameworks that produce poverty, exclusion, and social discrimination through the study of social and economic policies.

INSTITUTIONAL SPONSORS

THE LEGAL AGENDA

The Legal Agenda is a Beirut-based non-governmental non-profit organization that addresses issues of legal activism, reform, and transformation in the context of social and political change in the Arab world. It aims to challenge the conventional wisdom that the law is a "technical" matter of little social influence. This "technical" definition hinders public accountability, undermines a rights-based discourse of change, and dismisses legal activism as a tool for advancing the interests of disadvantaged groups in society.

ARAB STUDIES INSTITUTE

The Arab Studies Institute is a not-for-profit organization that produces knowledge on matters related to the Arab world and its relations. It serves as an institute in its own right and as an umbrella organization for five other subsidiaries: the *Arab Studies Journal*, *Jadaliyya*, *Quilting Point*, *FAMA* (Forum on Arab and Muslim Affairs), and *Tadween Publishing*.

ASFARI INSTITUTE FOR CIVIL SOCIETY AND CITIZENSHIP

The Asfari Institute for Civil Society and Citizenship, based at the American University of Beirut, seeks to advance research and other initiatives to support the development of an informed citizenry engaged at all levels of Arab associational life and promote openness, transparency, and accountability in the region.

Human Rights Non-Governmental Organizations in Egypt
Menna Omar

HISTORICAL BACKGROUND

The inception of Egyptian civil society dates back to 1821 when the first NGO, "The Greek Society," was formed in Alexandria.[1] The first wave of civil society organizations emerged from religious and charitable institutions that depended on Zakat and donations in general. Some researchers consider that these institutions belong to the first generation of NGOs in the Arab world. Today they constitute nearly sixty percent of the total number of NGOs in the Arab world.[2]

NGOs became more prevalent early in the twentieth century. Since their inception, they have been distinct from charity institutions, or those with a religious nature (whether Islamic or Christian). Charity institutions relied almost exclusively on local contributions, and expanded faster than NGOs, which relied mostly on foreign funding.[3] In 1923, the Egyptian constitution recognized people's right to assemble and form associations. Their numbers have increased greatly since then.[4]

Egyptian society and the regulation of its institutions have passed through several stages since that time. The government issued the first NGO law in 1945. It focused exclusively on regulating "charity associations, social institutions, and the manner of donation.[5]" During the Nasser era, the government considered civil activities as an extension of government activities and a portal for its policies. Legislation in this era focused on regulating civil activities and the right to assemble. In 1964, a new law placed civil associations and NGOs under total custody and administrative supervision.[6] The culture of restricting civil society organizations has become stronger ever since.

Starting in the 1980s, the government's practice for dealing with civil society organizations began to evolve as it saw them as part of the democratization process. This coincided with the government's interest in economic liberalization. As a result, the number of civil society organizations has risen considerably since the eighties.[7]

In 1991, the government established a Ministry of Social Consolidation/Social Affairs to supervise civil associations and NGOs. Eight years later, the Egyptian parliament passed a new law aimed at curbing civil society independence. This law sparked controversy and a direct confrontation between the government and civil society. In 2000, the Supreme Constitutional Court ruled the law unconstitutional based on both technical and substantive reasons. Then in 2002, the parliament passed a new law regulating civil society organizations and institutions which remains in effect today.

NGOS VERSUS CIVIL ASSOCIATIONS

Charity institutions mainly work on providing humanitarian services like providing medical relief as well as helping orphans and widows. In contrast, NGOs are

> Entities established by citizens in order to participate in public affairs through free and independent initiatives, whether on a limited local level or on a national, regional, or global one. In theory, NGOs are an expression of the will of society and citizens. Some NGOs take it upon themselves to spread principles of human rights and defend marginalized communities, while others work in the fields of development and poverty alleviation, and others tend to work in charity, and amongst all of this there are organizations concerned in providing services and humanitarian aid.[8]

NGOs are distinct from civil associations in that they are based on human rights and development whereas the latter primarily provide aid and relief. NGOs also monitor the government and act as a check on its authority to protect targeted groups from abuse and must, therefore, remain independent.

NGO CATEGORIES AND NUMBERS

Egyptian NGOs today cover a broad spectrum including women's rights, farmers' rights, labor, victims of torture to other groups. This report will focus on NGOs that are based on human rights principles and/or defend human rights.

There is no definite number of NGOs in Egypt because official statistics for them are unavailable. The researcher attempted to get a number from the Ministry of Solidarity but discovered that this required approval from the ministry's security office. Available numbers indicate that there are about 24,600 associations, institutions, and NGOs.[9]

OBSTACLES FACING NGOS

Article 22 of the International Covenant on Civil and Political Rights protects the right to form associations. The Egyptian Supreme Constitutional Court affirmed that people's right in forming civil associations is a part of their freedom of assembly in a ruling dated 3 June 2000. It emphasized the interlocking relationship between the freedom to form associations, the right to assemble, and freedom of expression. The court also added that the right to assemble is entwined with freedom of expression and forms one of the elements of personal freedom, which must not be "restricted unless through substantive and procedural means that are required by the constitution or guaranteed by the law; it is one of the rights that must not be marginalized or aborted." The 2013 Egyptian constitution guarantees the freedom of assembly in Article 73 and the right to form civil associations and institutions in Article 75.

Nonetheless, establishing an NGO in Egypt is not an easy matter, especially if the organization intends to work in the human rights field, as the current law imposes restrictions on the establishment and work of NGOs.

The 2002 NGO law imposed many restrictions on establishing and administering organizations. These include the administrational body's right to object to the names of the association's founders and even eliminate candidates it sees unsuitable for membership in the association's administrational council.[10] Human rights reports indicate that elimination of candidates reflects instructions from the state's security apparatus and not for reasons related to their eligibility to run or to criminal conviction involving honor and integrity.[11] This is the authorities' way of settling scores with its opponents: by preventing them from joining or establishing associations. This is a simple example of the unhealthy atmosphere for NGOs in Egypt. This report will discuss other violations of the freedom to establish associations committed by Egyptian authorities.

NGOs concerned with human rights issues have protested the Civil Associations Law on many occasions. They have called for legislative reform to ensure citizens' right to establish associations as well as the ability to enjoy a margin of independence from the state. These organizations proposed choosing new legal forms, distinct from civil associations, to afford them the freedom they require to function effectively, and to escape the authorities' restriction of their work.

NGOS AND THE 2011 REVOLUTION

Before the 2011 revolution, the fields in which NGOs worked included defending women's rights, labor rights, defending victims of torture through legal and psychological support, and prisoners of conscience through legal defense. Others worked on spreading a culture of human rights and raising citizens' awareness of their rights, especially the youth. Publications by these organizations exposed the Mubarak regime's violations as well as its deception concerning many issues such as the disappearance of torture in prisons, or its progress in establishing social equality. NGOs aimed to embarrass the regime in front of the international community, which in turn exercised pressure to bring about reforms. Strategic litigation cases, which were filed by several human rights centers, were a major driving force behind the adoption of many rights for Egyptian citizens, and represented a kind of monitoring of public policy and government decisions. On this basis, many Egyptians considered that human rights organizations participated, in one way or another, in the outbreak of the revolution. These organizations also had a role during the revolution, a role after the revolution, and a role as of the time of writing.

RESEARCH METHODOLOGY

HUMAN RIGHTS NGOS AS THE SUBJECT FOR THE RESEARCH

Due to the significantly large number of NGOs and civil associations in Egypt, the researcher had to limit the sample of organizations for this study. Human rights NGOs are an apt choice because of their developing role in Egyptian society in recent years and also because they were intermittently and regularly subject to government restrictions. These restrictions have increased since the revolution which has impacted their scope of activities and the number of associated personnel. In addition to this, because human rights NGOs receive foreign funding, the government has targeted them. The researcher interviewed a sample of human rights NGOs based on their popularity and advocacy agenda. Interviews were carried out with a number of these organizations.

INTERVIEWS

Human rights NGOs interviewed:

- Institution for Freedom of Thought and Expression, 7 March 2014
- Egyptian Center for Economic and Social Rights, 29 April 2014
- National Community for Human Rights, 8 May 2014
- Nazra for Feminist Studies, 27 April 2014
- Land Center, 5 May 2014
- Nadim Center for Rehabilitation of Victims of Violence and Torture, 29 April 2014
- Hisham Mubarak Law Center
- Andalus Institute for Tolerance and Anti-Violence Studies, 28 April 2014
- Association for Egyptians Against Religious Discrimination, 28 April 2014

Interviews with political movements and initiatives:

- Initiative for I Saw Harassment, 28 April 2014
- Movement for Egyptians Against Coal, 5 May 2014

In addition to the interviews, the researcher scrutinized the NGOs' publications as well as media coverage and scholarly reports about them.

PART I: LEGAL FORM OF HUMAN RIGHTS NGOS IN EGYPT

Some NGOs in Egypt take the default legal form, which is the "civil association" form. NGOs that take this form are mostly charity organizations that depend on donations from citizens and work on providing aid to citizens. A few human rights organizations take the form of civil associations, including the Nazra for

Feminist Studies Association[12] and the Movement for Egyptian Against Religious Discrimination.

To evade invasive state regulation, human rights NGOs refused to adopt this legal form. To operate with greater freedom, most human right NGOs establish themselves as non-profit law firms or non-profit civil firms. The first form makes it possible to file lawsuits and conduct regular attorney work while the latter lacks this capacity.

Hisham Mubarak Law Center, Institution for Freedom of Thought and Expression, Egyptian Center for Economic and Social Rights, and National Community for Human Rights are incorporated as non-profit law firms. These organizations are active in filing lawsuits and pursuing strategic litigation. It is worth mentioning that these institutions were established before the revolution, except for the National Community for Human Rights, which was established after the revolution, in 2012 to be precise.

The Andalus Institute for Tolerance and Anti-Violence, the Nadim Center for Rehabilitation of Victims of Violence and Torture, and the Land Center are incorporated as non-profit civil firms. Notably, the Nadim Center for Rehabilitation of Victims of Violence and Torture was registered as a non-profit civil firm due to its unique status; it was originally a medical clinic and registered with the Ministry of Health and Union for Doctors. They also have a license for medical clinics from the concerned authorities.[13]

When asked why they chose these legal forms, they replied that it is due to the law's imposition of numerous restrictions over the work of NGOs. They also cited the bad experiences that some organizations went through like prosecution from security authorities, the denial of establishment, or arbitrary dissolution. The Hisham Mubarak Law Center and the Egyptian Center for Economic and Social Rights stated that they chose the form of a non-profit law firm in direct protest of the law.

Organizations have repeatedly demanded that the law be amended to better facilitate the freedom of establishing associations and the freedom to assemble, while preserving the organizations' right to choose their activities without prosecution from security authorities, and avoiding the financial control they are subject to at the current time. They declared their willingness to adjust their status and register as NGOs should this amendment be adopted. However, none of the amendments to date have achieved any of the aforementioned.

NGOs objected to the bill that was referred from former President Mohamed Morsi to the Shura Council because of the continuity of the spirit of restriction, dominance, and administrative custody over NGOs.[14] The organizations also objected to the vague provisions of the law including general order or public morals; to the intervention in the associations' right to freely set their bylaws, work regulations, and method of forming elected commissions; and the establishment of a "coordinative committee" that has the right to accept or refuse association funding and therefore controls the association's activities.[15]

After the removal of Morsi, the parliament once again submitted a bill to regulate the work of civil society organizations; NGOs objected to that as well.[16] The bill proposed to maintain the coordinating committee, referred to above, and stipulated that it be formed from eight government bodies including a representative of the Interior Ministry and a representative of the National Security Authority. The bill prohibited associations from carrying out any field research or opinion polls without prior consent from the Central Agency for Public Mobilization and Statistics, which, on the one hand, reflects the government's ignorance of the nature of NGOs and, on the other, a desire for full control over their activities.

The bill also forbade the establishment of any institution that takes a legal form other than "civil association" and practices association work. This would effectively prohibit the legal forms that most human rights organizations currently assume, namely, non-profit legal firms and non-profit civil firms. In the case that they do not adjust their status and if they are under the jurisdiction of the Ministry of Social Affairs, the penalty is imprisonment of the founders and payment of a fine.[17] NGOs rejected this bill, and as of the time of writing, a new law for NGOs in Egypt has not been proposed.

In an attempt by the authorities to control these institutions, the Ministry of Social Solidarity published an advertisement in Al-Ahram newspaper on 22 July 2014, warning that it would dissolve all institutions that conduct civil work without a license from the ministry.[18] This directly threatened NGOs established as a non-profit legal or civil firm. In a memorandum sent to Prime Minister Ibrahim Mohleb, sponsoring organizations considered this edict a declaration of war by the government on the "freedom of establishing and activities of the civil society in Egypt, and a flagrant aggression on legal regulations that have been stable for a long time with respect to law firms and activities of developmental, academic and cultural nature."

The status of these organization remains unstable, as they wait to see whether the Ministry's warning is a mere threat or whether it materializes into something on the ground.

PART II: OBJECTIVES OF HUMAN RIGHTS NGOS IN EGYPT

The human rights organizations interviewed are concerned with several objectives. Egyptians Against Religious Discrimination seeks to promote freedom of thought and belief, defending the principle of citizenship, and criminalizing all forms of discrimination especially on the basis of religion. The Nazra for Feminist Studies Association aims to "form an Egyptian feminist movement that believes in the feminist cause and that social and gender trends are also political and impact the development and liberalization of societies." Nazra also works on incorporating the aforementioned causes in the public and private spheres of society.[19] In addition, Nazra seeks enhance the feminist movement by including new groups and incorporating youth groups.[20]

The Institution for Freedom of Thought and Expression aims to achieve freedom of thought and expression. Its secondary objectives stem from this general principle including academic freedom (like unfair dismissal and intervention in labor affairs), media freedom, creative freedom, the right to knowledge, and the right to exchange information. The institution considers the right to exchange information as central to all the aforementioned freedoms.

The main objective for the Institute for Tolerance and Anti-Violence Studies is based on spreading the culture of tolerance and citizenship in Egypt. The Egyptian Center for Economic and Social Rights seeks to empower Egypt's poor and to work with them in order to achieve economic and social rights on their behalf. It states that it is committed to giving society, in all of its groups, the power to enjoy its economic, social and cultural rights through reinforcing social movements that defend these rights, and awakening a new social movement that achieves the highest levels of participation, and is able to influence, change and spread the culture of human rights in general and the economic and social rights in particular, notably labor rights and union rights, in addition to defense campaigns, building coalitions, forming networks, providing legal assistance, and resorting to courts of law.[21]

The Hisham Mubarak Law Center is committed to confronting violations of human rights, providing all possible means of help for victims of these violations, activating judicial procedures and joint work efforts between institutions of civil society in order to drop laws that are incompatible with the principles of the constitution and human rights, prosecuting and punishing human rights violators, and providing judicial requirements to do justice for the victims of these violations.[22]

The Nadim Center for Rehabilitation of Victims of Violence and Torture seeks to eliminate all forms of violence and torture, in addition to supporting victims of violence and torture by all means possible, like providing medical help, psychological rehabilitation, or legal support.

The Egyptian Center for Economic and Social Rights focuses mainly on labor issues. The Land Center seeks to defend the rights of peasants and farmers and to enable them to defend their rights and interests on their own. The Egyptian Initiative for Personal Rights works on strengthening and protecting fundamental rights and freedoms in Egypt.[23] The Cairo Institute for Human Rights Studies articulates several objectives for its work: supporting the respect for principles of human rights and democracy; analyzing the difficulties of applying the international humanitarian law for human rights; spreading the culture of human rights in the Arab world; and strengthening the dialogue between cultures within the framework of international conventions and covenants for human rights. The National Committee for Human Rights, which was established in 2012, aims to build a base in society that would apply pressure to apply human rights.

Youth initiatives formed after the revolution work on specific causes. For example, the initiative of I Saw Harassment aims at opposing the sexual harassment phenomenon in Egypt through different means. The initiative of Egyptians Against Coal was created in the wake of the Egyptian government's guidance to use coal to generate power. It seeks to cultivate a popular base to resist this guidance.

From the above, we note that organizations are established for specific causes. Each one of them works in a field of specialization. Each organization's projects are set according to the field of work it is concerned with. For example, when counting the projects/departments that the Institution for Freedom of Thought and Expression works on, we notice that they are specialized projects that serve the main objective, which in turn is a narrow objective. This is the case for the rest of the organizations as well. The only organizations that does not specify a field is Hisham Mubarak Law Center, as it is concerned with human rights cases in general. An emphasis on legal rights is what best distinguishes this organization. It works on cases that fall within the scope of human rights in general like refugee cases, labor cases, freedom of opinion and expression, the right to demonstrate, and other rights and freedoms.

PART III: INTERNAL ORGANIZATIONAL STRUCTURE OF HUMAN RIGHTS NGOS IN EGYPT

This section discusses the internal organizational structure of the NGOs in question, their geographic distribution, the number of employees in these organizations before and after the revolution, and their funding policies.

INTERNAL ORGANIZATIONAL STRUCTURE

Most of the NGOs examined rely on an executive committee or a general assembly, which makes decisions on behalf of the institution. Their aim is to avoid decisions made on an individual basis and to listen to the ideas and aspirations of employees. These institutions try not to become too centralized and also try to reflect a model for the virtues of decentralization. To date, however, they have not been able to achieve this and remain centralized for the most part. The NGOs have not established elections inside their institutions to choose members of the executive bureau or the executive or administrative committee, or even to choose a representative for worker affairs in these committees. This reflects the scarcity of steps taken by these organizations to develop their internal organizational structure, and the need to take positive steps in order for the workers to have a role in choosing their representatives as well as the committees to manage the institution.

Some organizations rely on an executive bureau or executive committee to make important decisions for the institution; they are: Institution for Freedom of Thought and Expression, Nazra for Feminist Studies, and Egyptian Center for Economic and Social Studies. The executive bureau or the executive committee in the Egyptian Center for Economic and Social Studies and Nazra for Feminist Studies includes the executive manager, deputy executive manager, and projects managers or team leaders; they have a sound structure based on membership in the executive bureau from those who hold certain positions. The executive committee in the Institution for Freedom of Thought and Expression includes seven people appointed by the executive manager, deputy executive manager, and manager of the legal department. However, alongside the executive commission, workers at the Institution for Freedom of Thought and Expression hold periodic consultation meetings regarding problems the institution or workers are facing, or to consult regarding certain topics, in addition to encouraging participation in daily decision-making inside the institution.

The Hisham Mubarak Law Center and the National Committee for Human Rights depend on the general assembly model that includes all the workers in their association. The Hisham Mubarak Law Center's general assembly convenes once a year and is entrusted with the major decisions of the center like strategies and work plans. Some friends of the center are also invited for consultation and advice but do not have the right to vote. As for daily executive matters, there is an executive manager for the center who is the manager of the executive committee, which includes branch managers and one of the partners who has the right to sign, in addition to one of the project managers and the financial manager. In addition to all of that, workers at the Hisham Mubarak Center hold a meeting with the executive manager of the branch once a week to discuss work development, issues they are following up on, and any matters that come up during the week and require discussion. The organizations in question consider this method of decision-making to be optimum. We noticed that this model diminishes the need for hierarchy and increases participation by all workers in decision-making with a voting mechanism that ensures democracy inside the organization.

As for the National Committee for Human Rights, it is the only institution that declared that it is based on the principle of membership, as there are members in this committee that pay dues. All members of the National Committee constitute the general assembly, which elects the general secretary who forms the secretariat-general, which is the body authorized to take the executive role of the National Committee. The National Committee has chosen to have a specific structure to carry out executive matters; however this takes place through elections. In doing so, it made all its members participate in decision-making in an organized manner, even the workers whom it also considers members in the committee. Perhaps these membership and election models are due to the establishment of the institution based on the principles of human rights and the revolution. This reflects the development of youth movements and the institutions formed after the revolution, which have made more deliberate attempts to develop in the fields of representation, democracy, and decision-making.

SIZE OF HUMAN RIGHTS NGOS IN EGYPT

This section discusses the size of NGOs with respect to their distribution in governorates, the number of workers in them, and whether the number of workers in them increased after the revolution or stayed the same.

DISTRIBUTION OF HUMAN RIGHTS NGOS IN EGYPTIAN GOVERNORATES

Most NGOs do not have branches outside Cairo, and if they do have branches they are small or just a group of people to handle affairs that is connected in a centralist and hierarchal manner with the main branch in Cairo.

Examples of organizations that have branches outside Cairo include: the Hisham Mubarak Law Center, which has a branch in Aswan (south of Egypt); the Egyptian Center for Economic and Social Rights, which has a branch in the governorate of Alexandria; the Egyptian Initiative for Personal Rights, which has three offices: an office in Cairo to follow up on cases in greater Cairo, an office in Luxor to follow up on cases in Upper Egypt, and an office in Alexandria to follow up cases in the north-west of the Delta.

The rest of the institutions have representatives or people who follow up the cases in the governorates like the Institution for Freedom of Thought and Expression, which has an attorney in each governorate to legally represent it in that governorate and to follow up on cases it is working on. As for the newly formed youth movements, they also rely on the representatives in each governorate system. This may be due to their emphasis on grassroots organizing and their refusal to adopt an institutional structure.

Perhaps the concentration of NGOs in Cairo is not the choice of institutions, as they are concerned with reaching the greatest number of beneficiaries and working on the greatest number of cases. Instead, it could reflect the shortage of resources and the restrictions placed on them by government authorities.

NUMBER OF WORKERS IN HUMAN RIGHTS NGOS

NGOs rely on full-time employees, but they also rely on volunteers without pay. This is due to the nature of NGOs, which is based on human rights issues and public issues. Working in these organizations can be considered a "public service" for society.

Many organizations were volunteer-based in their inception. They then felt a need for a structure for the institution and full-time employees to follow up on work on a daily basis and to develop work. For example, Nazra for Feminist Studies was established in 2005 and had five individuals (men and women) under the age of thirty working as volunteers. They then saw a need to establish a civil association so there could be a structure, employees, and expansion of their work. It was registered as a civil association in 2007. Most of the institutions in questions were established in a modest way in the beginning and then later developed. This is due to an increase of financial resources or a growth of necessary work or both. We noticed that in most organizations the number of workers increased after the revolution for one of the two of the aforementioned reasons.

Most NGOs in Egypt are average in size. The largest center among the organizations in this sample, in regard to the number of workers, is the Andalus Institute for Tolerance and Anti-Violence Studies. It employs seventy individuals and has eighty volunteers. Similarly, the Egyptian Center for Economic and Social Rights has seventy paid workers, in addition to volunteers.

The Nadim Center for Rehabilitation of Victims of Violence and Torture, the Institute for Freedom of Thought and Expression, and Nazra for Feminist Studies stated that their number of workers increased after the revolution. The number in Nadim Center increased to twenty-seven people from twenty due to the increase of the number of doctors, psychologists, and workers in legal assistance, documentation, translation, and so on. The Institute for Freedom of Thought and Expression witnessed a gradual increase in the number of workers from 2011 to 2014, until the number of workers reached between thirty to thirty-five people at the time of writing. Nazra for Feminist Studies also witnessed a gradual increase in the number of workers. In 2010 the number of workers was only ten individuals, and they were not all full-time workers. In 2011 the number increased to eighteen people, and by 2014 it increased to thirty people.

On the other hand, newly formed youth movements rely on volunteer labor entirely. As they do not take the form of a civil association or a non-governmental organization, they cannot rely on funding in any shape or form; they depend on volunteering, in-kind donations, and contributions from members of the campaign. Most of the volunteers in these campaigns are young men and women who believe in the objectives of the campaign and seek change.

FUNDING POLICIES

Funding is critical to all the functioning of NGOs. Professor Salma Al-Naqqash stated that one reason for changing Nazra from a volunteer feminist group to a civil association was to be able to secure funding, as they saw that self-funding is not successful all the time.

All the institutions that we interviewed considered funding a kind of partnership with the financier institution. They also emphasized that they do not allow any intervention from the financier in choosing projects, policy of work, or activities and methods through which they are carried out. They present the project as a whole to the financier, who then has the choice to accept it or refuse it without any intervention or ownership.

Some of the institutions in question indicated their refusal to accept funding from certain bodies. Most organizations unanimously agreed on their refusal to receive funding from foreign governments and embassies (i.e. Nazra for Feminist Studies, Institution for Freedom of Thought and Expression, Nadim Center for Rehabilitation of Victims of Violence and Torture, National Committee for Human Rights, and Egyptian Center for Economic and Social Rights). The Andalus Center for Tolerance and Anti-Violence Studies does not refuse funding from specific bodies and instead sets the conditions of its acceptance of funding on a project-by-project basis and a guarantee of non-intervention.

Some of the NGOs refused receiving funds from US bodies. The Andalus Center did not refuse as it sets the criteria on a project basis as indicated. The Egyptian Center for Economic and Social Rights also indicated that it refuses funding from certain US bodies, but not all of them. For example, it refuses to receive funding from USAID, but it accepts it from the Open Society Foundation. It also declared that dealing with European organizations is easier because there is greater trust in their intentions.

Organizations stated that they prefer to deal with NGOs in the same field of work, where there is a greater likelihood of convergence in ideas and principles

PART IV: ADVOCACY TACTICS EMPLOYED BY HUMAN RIGHTS NGOS

Previous sections discussed the objectives of NGOs in Egypt. In order to achieve these objectives, these organizations pursue several advocacy tactics. This section examines the most important tactics employed by these organizations.

SPREADING KNOWLEDGE

NGOs spread knowledge through several tactics, including raising awareness by making people aware of their rights. Some organizations offer training on certain topics, which is also considered a kind of spreading knowledge. In addition, some NGOs have research units to produce research reports and studies.

Once a NGO produces knowledge, it spreads it through several means. For example, the Cairo Institute for Human Rights has a special program to teach human rights. In this program, they organize workshops and training sessions regarding topics concerned with human rights.[24] Workshops target Egyptian college students and the youth in general.

Some organizations have chosen to resort to modern means and the popular arts to teach human rights. For example, the Andalus Institute for Tolerance and Anti-Violence Studies teaches human rights through games, songs, movies, and various other methods. Nazra for Feminist Studies sees that one approach for achieving progress in the feminist movement is incorporating new methods for raising awareness. Their tactics include organizing workshops dedicated to tackling taboos; producing short films that grapple with patriarchy; and developing an interactive theater to deal with gender issues like explicating the difference between the social roles of men and women.

Some associations offer training to raise awareness and build capabilities. For example, the Nadim Center for Rehabilitation of Victims of Violence and Torture trains grassroots organizations in providing psychological and legal assistance. It also trains lawyers and doctors in writing medical and psychological reports. The Institute for Freedom of Thought and Expression provides students with workshops on their rights and freedoms. The Andalus Institute for Tolerance and Anti-Violence Studies trains media workers, or those interested in working in the media, on the media's obligations to human rights standards, the ethical and professional standards of journalism, as well as running workshops aimed at reducing sectarianism and racism. Nazra for Feminist Studies gives special attention to supporting the participation of women in organized political work by training them to work in politics through the "Academy of Political Participation of Women." It is distinct in its intention to spread knowledge as well as to support greater participation. This is considered one way organizations can change reality.

Research units in NGOs produce research studies for dissemination. Each organization produces research that reflects its specialization. For example, the Egyptian Center for Economic and Social Rights' publications focus on economic and social rights including labor rights, tax, justice, environment, health, and education. So is the case for the rest of the organizations interviewed.

LITIGATION

Many organizations interviewed employ legal strategies to defend the rights and freedom of specific citizens who suffer violations. They also employ strategic litigation mechanisms to address state or government policies regarding human rights and civic freedoms.

LEGAL DEPARTMENTS

Most organizations interviewed have a department that provides legal support through a network of lawyers who defend individuals as well as broader classes of people. The Hisham Mubarak Law Center has been a pioneer in establishing its own legal department to defend demonstrators and the wronged, free of charge. Many well-known lawyers in Egypt began their careers in this legal department and later established their own centers, like Khaled Ali, Tareq Abu Nasser, Hafez Abu Saada, and others. Currently, the following organizations engage in some sort of legal advocacy: the Hisham Mubarak Law Center, the Egyptian Center for Economic and Social Rights, the Institution for Freedom of Thought and Expression, and the Egyptian Initiative for Personal Rights. In 2008, lawyers working in the Hisham Mubarak Law Center together with other volunteer lawyers established the Front for Defending Demonstrators of Egypt. These lawyers defended many demonstrators who were arrested at different political events like those on 6 April 2008; those leading up to and through the 25 January revolution; and the events and demonstrations that came afterwards.

The Legal Empowerment Department at the National Committee for Human Rights provides legal assistance for people who have had their rights violated. There is also a Commercial Department that provides legal consultations in exchange for a fee for cases unrelated to human rights like establishing a company, writing contracts, and civil suits. This generates additional income for the NGO.

STRATEGIC LITIGATION

Strategic litigation means designing a lawsuit and taking it to court in order to reach change on both legal and social levels. Strategic litigation is based on protesting government policies either to restrain the government from implementing a policy or compel it to enact others it has failed to implement. Some organizations in question have resorted to court, especially administrative courts, to appeal government decisions or compel it to fulfill its duties. Below are a few cases that these institutions brought to court before and after the revolution.

For example, the Hisham Mubarak Law Center's strategic litigation cases have involved female genital mutilation; Egyptians abroad voting in elections after the revolution, which gave Egyptians living abroad the right to vote in referendums and elections; and cases of virginity tests conducted at administrative courts, which led to the suspension of this practice by the Military Council.

The Egyptian Center for Economic and Social rights worked on some cases related to the annulment of contracts to sell lands owned by the state; annulment of contracts to privatize public companies; and civil damages cases for people who were injured during the revolution.

Resorting to strategic litigations reflects the organizations' desire to change reality and go beyond raising awareness and issuing statements. These organizations go even further, as they empowering citizens (litigants) in the social justice transformation process as well.

NGOs pursue several advocacy methods on behalf of the most marginalized communities. These include coordinating campaigns to exercise pressure over the government, issuing reports and statements, and participating in international legal mechanisms like the Universal Periodic Review (UPR) before the Human Rights Committee. NGOs' advocacy has served as an opportunity to engender a public discussion about government laws and proposed bills.

The Hisham Mubarak Law Center has launched A Homeland Without Torture and No for Military Courts for Civilians campaigns. In 2010, before the revolution, the Andalus Institute for Tolerance and Anti-Violence Studies launched a campaign to oppose the death penalty.

In addition, these organizations issue statements and reports concerning government practices that fall within their scope of work. For example, the Egyptian Center for Economic and Social Rights issues statements related to labor boycotts and protests. The Institute for Freedom of Thought and Expression, issues statements regarding student rights, academic freedom, the right to knowledge, and other issues related to their mandate. The same applies for the rest of the institutions in question.

LOCAL AND INTERNATIONAL COALITIONS

Coalitions are considered a form of networking and coordination that impacts an organization's efficacy. Coalitions are voluntary-based relationships between a group of institutions that agree on a number of principles or work in the same field.

NGOs in Egypt have joined several local and international coalitions. A local coalition is usually formed to work on a specific cause on a short- or long-term basis. This is considered a form of cooperation, networking, and coordination between these organizations. Generally speaking, local coalitions are not considered to have an institutional nature but rather maintain an ad-hoc one based on achieving specific tasks.

Short-term local coalitions may or may not be limited to a specified period. For example, Nazra for Feminist Studies, the Cairo Institute for Human Rights, and the Egyptian Association for the Arousal of Social Participation have cooperated in monitoring elections since 2010 in what is called the Independent Coalition to Monitor Elections. They divide the work among them to monitor elections from different perspectives, each according to their field of specialization. Also, the Andalus Institute for Tolerance and Anti-Violence Studies cooperates with the Egyptian Coalition for Monitoring Elections regarding monitoring and media coverage.

In March 2011, feminist organizations established a coalition to work on a legislative and constitutional agenda related to women-specific issues. Separately, there exists a coalition to organize a celebration for International Women's Day. It is meant solely for this task and is active in March of each year.

There is also a human rights coalition dedicated to submitting a UPR submission on Egypt's compliance with human rights law, which is only active during the time it is preparing and submitting this submission.

Egyptian NGOs also enter into regional and international organizations related to their mandate. The Egyptian Center for Economic and Social Rights, for example, is a member of the Arab Non-Governmental Organizations for Development, the Network of Migrant Labor in the Middle East, the Network for Tax Justice in Africa, in addition to maintaining continuous coordination with organizations that work in labor issues in Arab countries.

The Institution for Freedom of Thought and Expression has joined the IVECS network, which is an international network that includes organizations for freedom of opinion and expression. The institution is also a member in the African Court on Human and People's Rights.

The Nadim Center for Rehabilitation of Victims of Violence and Torture is a member of the Salma Network and the Aisha Network, both dedicated to women's rights. As for torture cases, the NGO is a member of MENA Regional Network, which includes organizations working in the rehabilitation of victims of torture in the Middle East and North Africa, and the IRCT network for centers working in the rehabilitation of victims of torture but on an international level. It includes around 170 organizations. Nazra for Feminist Studies has joined the International Coalition for Female Defenders of Human Rights.

PART V: RELATIONSHIP BETWEEN HUMAN RIGHTS NGOS

A pertinent question regarding Egyptian human rights NGOs is how they collaborate with one another. Do they, for example, cooperate together or do they compete for work and workers?

COOPERATION: THE DOMINANT FEATURE OF THE WORK OF HUMAN RIGHTS NGOS

Interviews with NGOs revealed the lack of uniformity among Egyptian civil society. To the contrary, it is quite diverse and vast. It includes charity organizations, developmental organizations, and human rights organizations. Accordingly, cooperation and competition cannot be assessed broadly. This analysis will be limited to cooperation among human rights NGOs.

Human rights NGOs indicated that the dominant feature in their interaction is cooperation. This does not mean there is no competition; however, it is a competition to achieve progress. Competition does not take the form of fierce competition, as each organization has a specific field of specialization. To the extent that competition exists, it is limited to organizations that work in the same field.

As for competition for workers in these organizations, there is a natural competition. For example, many workers in Hisham Mubarak Law Center move on, after a period of time, to work in another organization that can provide a more competitive salary. This is a natural phenomenon in all fields.

DEALING WITH NEWLY FORMED ORGANIZATIONS

In regard to their views on organizations and initiatives formed after the revolution, the NGOs interviewed unanimously agreed on their total support for the right to organize as an essential element for reconstituting the state. They also welcomed all initiatives and organizations regardless of their organizational form. They indicated that establishing these initiatives is considered a positive development because Egyptian society has many outstanding needs.

Ms. Salma Al-Naqqash from Nazra for Feminist Studies, indicated that her association supported several groups formed in governorates to work on women's causes like Free Southern Women in Aswan, These Ladies (honna) in Assiut, Don't be Quiet in Sohag, and Throttled in Mahalla. Nazra established these groups to close a sustainability gap and capture organic grassroots energy. To this end, Nazra cooperated with them to build their capacity for pursuing the causes and priorities they adopt in their local societies, and to provide special resources, especially financial, even in the absence of a civil association.

The National Committee for Human Rights, which was formed after the revolution, indicated its legal support for the group No Military Courts for Civilians, demonstrating cooperation among organizations.

Mr. Osama Khalil from the Hisham Mubarak Law Center indicated that the only negative matter that may face these organizations and initiatives in the coming period, is that if work demand stagnates as it did during the Mubarak regime; this will lead to a scarcity of cases and resources to address them among organizations. In this case, the solution would be networking between these organizations, joint ventures, or the merger of some organizations.

FORUM OF INDEPENDENT NGOS: A MODEL OF PRIORITIZING A COMMON INTEREST

Egyptian NGOs often issue joint statements and collaborate on joint campaigns. NGOs consider such joint advocacy as an effective tool to confront governing authorities.

Under the Mubarak regime, a so-called Forum of Independent NGOs was established to confront the Mubarak regime's tactics aimed at co-opting existing NGOs and creating new ones to serve its interests. These organizations, which the regime created, issued reports surrounding the status of human rights in Egypt that contradicted reality. This necessitated cooperation between independent NGOs to confront them. The forum is a space for a large group of organizations to coordinate tactics and adopt common positions. They take the lead on submitting the UPR on behalf of Egyptian NGOs. These organizations are active in issuing joint statements surrounding administrative decisions, government practices, legal and constitutional decrees related to their respective fields of work, and judicial orders. The Forum emphasizes civil and political rights in their statements.[25] The number of organizations issuing joint statements has reached twenty-three. This number varies depending on the subject of the statement. Cooperation between these organizations has enhanced their leverage and increased their visibility among TV and print news media following the revolution.

Notably this coalition is not traditional in that it lacks a hierarchy. The door is open for member as well as non-member organizations to attend the sessions. When a meeting is held to make a decision, it is announced so that all those concerned can attend. Evidence of the coalition's successful organizing model is that no organizations that have withdrawn from it so far.[26]

PART VI: THE REVOLUTION AND HUMAN RIGHTS NGOS

DID THE WORK OF NGOS CONTRIBUTE TO THE OUTBREAK OF THE REVOLUTION?

With regard to the outbreak of the revolution, NGOs do not give themselves any credit. They even emphasize that the revolutionary moment was a spontaneous one. However, members of these organizations acknowledged that they saw people who attended their training sessions and workshops involved in the revolution. This indicates that these organizations had a role, although a minimal one, in the outbreak of the revolution by spreading the culture of human rights and raising the citizens' awareness of their rights. Some people believe that the youth who participated in the revolution developed their critical political consciousness at the hands of human rights NGOs, through their training sessions, workshops, and travel abroad to events and conferences. Even before the revolution, Egypt witnessed movements like the labor one taking a similar initiative. For example, they exposed election fraud in the 2010 parliamentary elections. They have also documented violations, exposed them to the public, brought lawsuit, and supported labor strikes. This exposure of human rights violations as a part of public engagement had a major role in the outbreak of the revolution.

The case of Khaled Sa'id, which some consider one of the main catalysts for the revolution, was a case to which the organizations contributed, especially the Nadim Center. They published a report, issued statements, and highlighted conditions in prisons and the systematic use of torture. Organizations' work in strategic litigation contributed to raising people's awareness that they are engaged in a campaign for enhancing their rights and, in the process, they demonstrated the efficacy of civil society participation.

During the revolution, these organizations and their employees participated in demonstrations. In addition, these organizations made their offices available for protestors and organizers. They opened up their spaces to receive citizens' donations of food and goods to be distributed to people at sit-ins and demonstrations. Additionally, these organizations provided direct services like volunteer medical services in field hospitals.

These organizations also contributed to the massive demonstrations on 30 June 2013. They published reports exposing the human rights violations committed by the Muslim Brotherhood regime. They also monitored the government's work practices and policies. This had an impact in raising people's awareness, which in turn had an impact on people's protest to these practices.

How the Revolution of 25 January Affected NGOs

After the revolution of 25 January, Egyptian society benefitted from the lifting of many restrictions that had been imposed on its liberty. Accordingly, this had an impact on NGOs, their tactics, methods of work, priorities, and funding, and it increased the number of employees.

Generally speaking, the public sphere became more open after the revolution. This increased the opportunities for new NGOs as well as youth groups that did not take the form of NGOs. Youth initiatives employed tools and methods distinct from those used by NGOs. For example, youth initiatives used graffiti, interactive theater, and worked extensively in social media. Many organizations similarly developed their tools to keep pace with developments taking place. In this context, a boom occurred regarding the use of social networking for raising awareness and advocacy campaigns.

In the course of this new activism, new issues arose. For example, the increased presence of women in large numbers in the public sphere demanded new advocacy initiatives. To this end, Nazra for Feminist Studies established the Political Participation Academy for Women in September 2011 to support the presence of women in organized political work.

The liberalization of the political field after the revolution created a need for NGOs to monitor elections to ensure their compliance with integrity and transparency standards. The state also responded differently to the role of

NGOs in elections. Before the revolution, the state did not readily accept this monitoring; however, after the revolution, the Supreme Committee for Elections became more inclusive to organizations that wished to monitor elections. This is due to the Egyptian society's desire to conduct fair and transparent elections, the state's desire to assure society that it was trustworthy, and the international community's scrutiny of Egypt and its political process in particular. The international community depended on NGO reports on elections, and the state was invested in demonstrating good will and compliance. The state's good will also encouraged NGOs to engage in new decision-making processes. These included social dialogue between NGOs and government entities. For example, the state permitted NGOs to organize delegations to visit prisons in an effort to demonstrate its commitment to human rights to the international community. While the state was open to these delegations and the reports that resulted from them, it did little to nothing to implement its recommendations. It was more concerned with developing an image of human rights compliance without substance.

In addition, some new problems and challenges in society emerged which necessitated the expansion in projects and fields of work on part of these organizations. Organizations that had worked on women's causes in the private sphere became more interested in similar causes in the public sphere. For example, harassment of women in public spaces dominated discussions about women after the revolution. It has become one of the most important cases on the agendas of feminist organizations. Many youth movements formed after the revolution are similarly concerned with harassment. For example, movements were established like I Saw Harassment, Harassmap, Your Hands Off, Homeland Without Harassment, and other campaigns and initiatives. In response to the difference between harassment at demonstrations and daily harassment that women suffer, in terms of severity and violence, which in some cases reaches assault and rape, these initiatives have adopted work mechanisms that are totally different from those that were adopted by NGOs. These initiatives work mostly on the ground by creating groups of volunteers who have the authority to make their own decisions, as they themselves set up all concepts and information, a field map for work, media policy, and other matters. This lent itself to creative approaches as indicated in the I Saw Harassment one. These volunteer groups were present at demonstrations and protected women from harassment and assault, which exposed them to danger and physical assault in many cases. In the same context, due to the severity of assaults against women in the public sphere, the Nadim Center for Rehabilitation of Victims of Violence and Torture included these women under a program called Violence Against Women to rehabilitate them psychologically.

Like the increase of assaults against women, there was a general rise in violence against demonstrators in the form of arrests, injuries and killings. This also had its impact on NGOs in Egypt, as the number of cases that they worked on increased. Cases of arrests of demonstrators especially necessitated the increase of lawyers and organizations working on these issues. For example, the Institution for Freedom of Thought and Expression stated that it had set up a network of lawyers so that there existed a lawyer in each governorate who represents the institution to respond to the high number of cases. They also established new programs after the revolution like the project for freedom of creativity and the project for digital freedom. The Nadim Center for Victims of Violence and Torture, for example, went to the morgue to be present during autopsies of demonstration victims to protect against fraud and foul play.

The revolution also affected foreign funding for NGOs. Foreign financiers increasingly dedicated grants to countries where revolutions took place, including Egypt. Funding had an impact on expanding projects and increasing the number of employees in these institutions.

THE OFFENSIVE AGAINST HUMAN RIGHTS NGOS AFTER 30 JUNE 2013

After the demonstrations of 30 June 2013, the work of NGOs was negatively affected. Their work became mainly focused on releasing detainees from prisons and fighting new laws restricting freedoms, especially the demonstration law.

Most of the interviewed NGOs issued statements that criticized the dispersal of a sit-in by the Muslim Brotherhood in Raba'a Square. They blamed the state for the killings and injuries at these events. Their criticism of state authorities heightened in regards to decisions and practices since the collapse of the Muslim Brotherhood regime. They described these tactics using terms like "repression" and "restriction of freedom" and other expressions that reflect the current regime's lack of respect for human rights as well as its intention to wage a war against the revolution of 25 January and its symbols.

The state also launched a war against these NGOs. The Egyptian Center for Economic and Social Rights was stormed twice after 30 June 2013. The first time was on 18 December 2013,[27] the second was on 22 May 2014 when the Alexandria branch was stormed after it organized a solidarity press conference with respect to the Mahyanoor Al-Masri case at the organization's headquarters.[28] In a development of the conflict between the state and NGOs, on 18 July 2014, the Ministry of Solidarity published an advertisement in Al-Ahram newspaper warning NGOs that are not registered as civil associations to adjust their status or risk being dissolved and legal prosecution of their founders and representatives.[29] The organizations considered the ministry's warning a declaration of war and a violation of the freedom of the right to assembly and association in Egypt.

This step by the Ministry of Solidarity reflects the anxiety that these organizations cause for the state, and the state's attempt to contain them. If it cannot do so, then getting rid of them is the solution. This demonstrates the influence of these organizations on the local and the international levels.

Professor Fat'hi Farid, from the I Saw Harassment Initiative, sees that the current regime's attempt to eliminate civil society is because it wants to eliminate the front that supports the revolutionary activists and those who are demanding their rights. After that, the elimination of the rest of those who are demanding their rights becomes easy since eliminating civil society is the key to empowering the corrupt.

Twenty-three human rights organizations presented a memorandum to the prime minister in which they objected to the law being drafted by the Ministry of Social Consolidation and to the warning published in Al-Ahram newspaper.[30] They also sought to start a dialogue with the government to cancel the warning; these efforts were fruitless. Because of these threats, seven independent human rights organizations decided not to participate in the activities of the Egyptian portfolio for human rights at the United Nations.[31]

On the other hand, and in order to confront the government's rhetoric and to defend the role of civil society, several human rights organization launched a campaign in October 2014 and called it Civil Society is a Right for You and Me. It aimed at breaking the barrier put by the government between the concept of civil society and common people before the deadline set by the ministry.[32]

The ministry announced on 11 November 2014, one day after the deadline, that it will study the case of each organization individually and correspond with it directly to comply with the 2002 law for civil associations and institutions. Human rights NGOs issued a statement demanding the government to open a "serious and transparent" dialogue regarding the role of civil society organizations.[33] The government remained unresponsive to this demand and a state of tension came to dominate the relationship between human rights NGOs and the Egyptian government. This caused the Cairo Center for Human Rights Studies to move its regional and international programs abroad because of the restrictions on the public domain as announced in a statement issued on 9 December 2014.

This state of restrictions puts the NGOs under constant threat, which affects, in one form or another, their activities especially in the long term. Up to the time of writing, these organizations continue their work and continue to file lawsuits related to political rights such as the cases of detained demonstrators.

PART VII: HUMAN RIGHTS NGOS AND POLITICS

The work of human rights NGOs occasionally comes into contact with political issues. This section will discuss the relationship between human rights NGOs and politics by discussing the background of their founders, if the organizations lean toward a political vision, the intertwinement of human rights issues with political issues, and the organizations' relationship with parties and unions.

The Organizations' Political Inclination

When asked about their political inclination, and whether they lean towards a party or camp, the organizations all responded that they do not have any political ideology. They also stated that their employees have different political ideologies, as they include leftists, liberals, as well as other political affiliations. In addition, founders of these NGOs are known for their human rights activities and not for their political activities.

For example, Hisham Mubarak, who established the Center for Legal Assistance for Human Rights, which later came to be known as Hisham Mubarak Law Center, is a prominent human rights lawyer and obtained an international prize in the human rights field in 1993.[34] Ahmed Saif Al-Islam, the executive manager of Hisham Mubarak Center, is a well-known human rights lawyer who handled the defense of many prisoners of conscience.[35] Also, Imad Mubarak, founder of the Institution for Freedom of Thought and Expression, was a human rights activist and a lawyer at Hisham Mubarak Center before he established the institution.

The NGOs interviewed consider themselves subject to human rights standards, as they are "human rights activists." Therefore, human rights standards govern their actions. This is a clear and deliberate distinction between an individual's affiliation and the organization as a juridical person. The National Committee for Human Rights adds that the principles of the revolution are essential principles that constitute their own ideological orientation. Of the organizations that were deeply affected by their founder's affiliation to a political orientation and activities, was the Egyptian Center for Economic and Political Rights. Its founder, Khaled Ali, worked in politics after the revolution by nominating himself for presidential elections in 2012 and established a political party as well. In order to maintain the center's neutrality and independence from politics, Ali resigned from it before the elections; although he retained a non-employee role as a counselor for the center. Nevertheless, the NGO is still connected to the name Khaled Ali.

Nazra for Feminist Studies considers feminism an ideology, a comprehensive intellectual system, as well as a political discourse and movement. The institution mentioned that the only thing for which they have a distinct position is the admission of some women in the "Academy of Political Participation of Women," which seeks to empower marginalized women in politics. As such, they did not accept all women into the academy because they did not receive women from the National Party or any entity affiliated with it because they possess considerable potential on their own. Similarly, they did not accept female Islamists who also possess considerable potential and, more than that, do not believe in the women's causes adopted by feminist movements.

The Andalus Institute for Tolerance and Anti-Violence Studies do not work with any organization or political formation that accepts violence as a legitimate tactic, because that contradicts its mandate. Dr. Magda Al-Adli, from Nadim Center for Rehabilitation of Victims of Violence and Torture, explained that the organizations' stance against Mubarak's regime and against the Muslim Brotherhood regime, stems from a commitment to feminism and human rights. Mubarak's regime violated human rights and the freedom of expression. The same was true for Morsi's regime, which violated many human rights, and adopted a political vision that would regress the achievement of women's rights.

The human rights NGOs interviewed deal with human rights standards as an ideology in and of itself. Aside from their employees who may adhere to a particular political orientation, the NGOs themselves remain politically independent and defend all the wronged, the poor, the marginalized, and others regardless of their political affiliation.

Perhaps the choice to separate politics from their human rights activities is due to the fact that they seek to appeal to different groups of Egyptian society. This choice is also explained perhaps by the fact that they seek to avoid accusations that they are implementing a specific political agenda. This was the optimal choice for these organizations in order not to confuse their roles with the roles of political parties, in addition to the fact that it is better for them to be independent of the regime as well as political ideologies. This enables them to monitor government performance, parliamentary performance, and other state institutions regardless of the prevailing political current.

JOINT STATEMENTS BY HUMAN RIGHTS ORGANIZATIONS: HUMAN RIGHTS AND POLITICS

Some statements issued by the organizations can be regarded as statements with a political inclination. For example, those that are related to the dispersal of sit-ins or decisions issued by the state like using coal to generate power, or those in response to judicial rulings against opponents of the regime, which can be seen as politically charged.

However, the NGOs do not consider these statements as political statements but rather human rights statements. The NGOs are concerned with issues that have a human rights nature, and when they issue a statement regarding a governmental decision or practice, it is directly related to one of the human rights or freedoms. They also consider that in many cases there is a relationship between human rights and politics. However this does not mean that they are involved in politics or that they are biased towards one political project. They do not adopt, for example, a bill due to an ideological policy but rather to its adherence to international standards and its commitment to citizens' rights.

The Relationship Between Human Rights Organizations and Parties and Unions.

NGOs regularly coordinate with political parties and unions on joint campaigns, statements, support for demands, or other things.

The Egyptian Center for Economic and Social Rights' work on labor rights naturally leads it to deal with unions. They deal with them as essential partners and, as such, they launch campaigns and joint demands in public affairs. The center also provides them with legal assistance as a matter of policy. Unions provide information for the center concerning violations committed, whether in regard to union or worker rights. This includes information about arbitrary dismissal from work or the violation of workers' rights to strike and so forth. In turn, the center provides information about issues relevant to these unions, like the right to assemble and strike.

Similarly, the Hisham Mubarak Law Center provides training for newly-formed independent unions. The National Committee for Human Rights provides legal support for some unions as well. The Nadim Center for the Rehabilitation of Victims of Violence and Torture mainly deals with the Union for Doctors as they are also members of this union. Sometimes they cooperate with the Union for Lawyers regarding bills concerning public health.

The relationship between human rights NGOs and unions is primarily based on cooperation over shared concerns. However, the organizations do not intervene in any way or form in union elections, as they do not support or reject any person.

With respect to parties, the organizations indicated that cooperation with parties mainly focuses on supporting parties or bills adopted, or demanded, by civil society. For example, provisions related to torture, sexual violence, domestic violence against women, and other laws.

The Egyptian Center for Economic and Social Rights declared that it maintains a cooperative relationship with six parties. It cooperates with them in certain campaigns related to economic and social rights. They also prompt them to adopt issues related to economic policies and economic and social rights. These parties are the Alliance Party, the Social Democratic Party, the Constitution Party, the Strong Egypt Party, the Egyptian Current Party, the Bread and Freedom Party, in addition to political movements such as the April 6 Movement and the Revolutionary Socialists.

The Hisham Mubarak Law Center provides skills-based training for newly-formed parties.

CONCLUSION

Human rights NGOs in Egypt have a noticeable impact on Egyptian society. Their concern with state abuses has engendered hostility from the government, which seeks to either contain or eliminate them. Currently, the NGOs are playing the role of the "wise man" in society. Increased polarization in Egyptian society often leads to extremism towards a certain idea or against a certain group. This has been the case with the Muslim Brotherhood at the time of writing as well as against some activists who were accused of conspiracy and betrayal. As such, human rights statements issued by these NGOs in protest are often considered as politicized and biased. In the context of the intensifying polarization from which Egypt currently suffers, tension will continue to increase between the organizations and the authorities, especially as NGOs continue to demand the release of detainees, fair trials for all prisoners even those affiliated with those Muslim Brotherhood, and reject the demonstration law, and the usage of coal to generate power and other governmental decisions and practices.

The first step in improving the relationship between the authorities and NGOs is the complete cessation of accusations that NGOs and their supporters are carrying out foreign agendas and receiving foreign funding for that purpose.

The state should cease its movement to adopt the NGOs bill and adhere to NGOs' demands to ensure the right to organize. The law should permit organizations to be established by notification, rather than by declaration. The law should also regulate membership in these organizations and facilitate acceptance of donations from within Egypt. The Egyptian Center for Economic and Social Rights indicated that the current law does not regulate receiving domestic funding; therefore, they must resort to appealing for foreign funding. Regulating domestic funding and membership will provide a means to sustain these organizations in addition to allowing the local society to merge with these organizations. On the other hand, it will also facilitate interventionist monitoring with the potential to impede the day to day affairs of the NGO.

Simultaneously, NGOs must continue to raise awareness in order for the citizens to understand the real role of NGOs and why they receive foreign funding. Notably, Egyptian society stands to benefit from learning about the entwined roles of the state, unions, parties, localities, parliamentarians, and NGOs. This needs a true effort on the part of the NGOs and not just through media activism.

In addition, the NGOs should reevaluate their internal decision-making mechanisms to afford more participation and freedom to their employees. This could include permitting employees to elect their representatives in the executive committee or relying on a general assembly that includes all the workers in the institution to determine the institution's strategies and to make important decisions.

QUESTIONS ASKED IN THE INTERVIEWS WITH HUMAN RIGHTS NGOS

1. When was the organization established and why? Who established the organization? Did they have any political or legal role before the establishment of the organization? (Historical background surrounding the organization).

2. What is the legal status of the organization? (Registrations status) Why was this type of registration chosen?

3. What are the objectives and strategies of the organization? Was this modified or developed after the revolution?

4. Does the organization rely on international law in its work? If so, how?

5. What is the number of workers in the organization? Do all of them work full time, or are there volunteers? Did this number change (whether increase or decrease) after the revolution?

6. What alliances has the organization joined, whether locally, regionally, or internationally?

7. Does the organization adopt a funding policy? Who are the main financiers? How do you regard funding?

8. How do you evaluate the work amongst the institutions of civil society in Egypt? Does competition prevail in projects and funding, or do coordination and networking prevail?

9. How do you evaluate the current alliance between the organizations of civil society regarding issues of a political and human rights nature? How do you explain this alliance? Why was it established and when? When did your organization join it?

10. Does the organization have any political inclination or affiliation?

11. What is the nature of the relationship between the organization on the one hand and unions and political parties on the other?

12. How do you evaluate the experience of NGOs in Egypt before and after the revolution?

13. Do you think that NGOs had a role in the eruption of the revolution? What is their role at the current time?

14. How do you explain the establishment of a number of civil society organizations and youth movements in Egypt after the revolution? Does this affect civil society in Egypt in a positive or negative manner?

15. How do you regard the role of civil society organizations in Egypt in the upcoming period?

16. In your opinion, what are the necessary things for the role of civil society in Egypt to be more effective?

ENDNOTES

[1] Amani Kandil, "An Attempt to evaluate the development of Arab civil society", in Bahgat Korany (ed), *The changing Middle East, A new look at regional dynamics*, The AUC Forum for International Affairs Edition, The American University in Cairo Press, 2010

[2] Amani Kandil,"An Attempt to evaluate the development of Arab civil society", in Bahgat and Korany (ed),*The changing Middle East, A new look at regional dynamics*, The AUC Forum for International Affairs Edition, The American University in Cairo Press, 2010.

[3] Mona Attia, "The Arab Republic of Egypt", in Barbara Lethem Ibrahim and Dina H.Sherif (eds.), *From Charity to Social Change*, The American University In Cairo Press, 2008.

[4] According to the website of the State Information Service.

[5] *Legislative development for NGOs in Egypt from 1938 to 1952*, The Egyptian Center for Public Politics Studies.

[6] Issam Addin Muhammed Hasan, *Towards a Democratic Law to Liberate Civil Activities – A Legal and Field Study*, The Cairo Center for Human Rights Studies, February 2009.

[7] Mohamed ElAgati, "Undermining Standards of good governance: Egypt's NGO's law and its impact on the transparency and Accountability of CSOs," in the *International Journal of Not-For-Profit law*, Volume 9, Issue 2, April 2007.

[8] *Non-Governmental Organizations*, Dr. Yousri Mustafa, published by Cairo Institute for Human Rights Institute, 2007.

[9] Amani Kandil,"An Attempt to evaluate the development of Arab civil society," paper published in "The changing Middle East, A new look at regional dynamics," The AUC Forum for International Affairs Edition, The American University in Cairo Press, 2010.

[10] Article 8 of the law.

[11] Issam Al-Din Muhammed Hasan, *Towards a Democratic Law to Liberate Civil Work – A Legal and Field Study*, published by Cairo Institute for Human Rights in February 2009.

[12] Based on an interview with Salma Al-Naqqash from Nazra for Feminist Studies, on 27 April 2014.

[13] Based on an interview with Dr. Majda Adli from Nadim Center for Rehabilitation of Victims of Violence and Torture.

[14] *The New Bill for Civil Associations and Institutions: Tangible Development and Inherited Disadvantages*, published 28 May 2012.

[15] *Muslim Brotherhood Lays the Foundation for a New Police State and Develops the Mechanisms of Mubarak's Regime in Suppressing Civil Work*, a joint statement issued by several NGOs, published on 30 May 2013.

[16] *The Bill for Civil Associations Subjugates Them Under the Control of the Government and Security Authorities*, joint statement issued by several NGOs, published 9 July 2014.

[17] Ibid.

[18] Memorandum sent by twenty-three human rights organizations to Prime Minister Ibrahim Mohleb on 24 July 2014.

[19] Website of Nazra for Feminist Studies www.nazra.org

[20] Based on an interview with Salma Al-Naqqash – Nazra for Feminist Studies on 27 April 2014.

[21] Website for Egyptian Center for Economic and Social Rights www.eccsr.org

[22] Website for Hisham Mubarak Law Center. www.hmlc-egy.org

[23] Website for Egyptian Initiative for Personal Rights www.eipr.org

[24] Official website for Cairo Institute for Human Rights Studies www.cihrs.org

[25] According to what Mr. Nadim Mansour, executive manager of Egyptian Center for Economic and Social Rights, stated in his interview on 29 April 2014.

[26] According to what Mr. Ahmed Samih, manager of Andalus Institute for Tolerance and Anti-Violence Studies, in his interview on 28 April 2014.

[27] *Abuse of Human Rights Organizations and the Return to What is Worst than Before 25 January 2011*, published on the website for the Egyptian Center for Economic and Social Rights on 19 December 2013.

[28] *Storming the Egyptian Center for the Second Time by the Current Regime, New Eras for Repressions,* published on the website for the Egyptian Center for Economic and Social Rights on 22 May 2014. And also *Grace of a Lifetime, Storming the Egyptian Center for Its Participation in Defending an Activist: A Continuation of the Series of Violations of Freedom of Expression and Fair Trials,* published on the website for the Legal Agenda on 24 May 2014.

[29] *Memorandum to Prime Minister Dr. Ibrahim Mohelb from 23 Human Rights Organizations,* on 24 July 2014.

[30] "Twenty-three Human Rights Organizations Demand the Government to Stop its Fight Against the Civil Society and to Reconsider its Policies," published on the website of the Cairo Center for Human Rights Studies, 24 July 2014.

[31] "Due to Threats to Human Rights Organizations, Seven Human Rights Organizations Decide not to Participate in the Activities of the Egyptian Portfolio in Egypt at the United Nations," published on the website of the Egyptian Initiative for Personal Rights, 4 November 2014.

[32] "Human Rights Organizations Launch a Campaign Called 'A Right for You and Me,' to Introduce the Role of Civil Society," published on the website for the Egyptian Initiative for Personal Rights, 23 October 2014.

[33] "Ten Human Rights Organizations Call for a Serious and Transparent Dialogue with the Government," published on the website of the Egyptian Initiative for Personal Rights, 18 November 2014.

[34] Safaa Srour, *Saif, Hisham, Fat'hi, and Al-Hilali: The Four Imams of Freedom,* published on the website of Al-Masri Al-Yom newspaper on 30 August 2014.

[35] Taqi Omar, *Death of the Attorney Fighter Ahmed Saif Al-Islam, One of the Pillars of the Human Rights Movement in Egypt,* published on the website of the Legal Agenda on 28 August 2014.

Associations in Tunisia after 14 January 2011 Study

Wahid Al-Farshishi

With contributions by Hanaa Bin Abduh & Khalid Al-Majri

INTRODUCTION

The role of civil society in Tunisia has witnessed remarkable development since January 2011, the date which marked the end of twenty-three years of dictatorship. The sequence of important events that the country is going through on all levels has contributed to highlighting the significance of this role, especially its significance in transitional periods like the one the Republic of Tunisia is currently experiencing.

Certain components of civil society played a direct role in the events that led to the fall of the former regime.

ROLE OF CIVIL SOCIETY

Certain components of civil society played an active and direct role in the events that led to the end of the former regime, as the intervention of the Tunisian General Labor Union (the leading labor organization in the country) and the National Association for Lawyers created a turning point for the course of events at the time. This role has continued in the different stages that Tunisia has been going through since 14 January 2011.

These components have had an important role and a big influence on all political, social, and legal levels of Tunisia's experience since that date, and this impact continues to this day:

- Components of civil society (traditional or revolutionary) participated in negotiations and debates that led to the formation of all the consecutive governments from 14 January 2011, leading up to the election of the Constituent Assembly and the emergence of the first government from this assembly in December 2011.

- Components of civil society participated in all the committees and associations that were formed after 14 January 2011, especially the High Commission for Achieving the Goals of the Revolution, Political Reform, and Democratic Transition; the National Committee for Investigating Bribery and Corruption; the National Committee for Investigating Encroachments on Record starting 17 December to the date of the expiration of the cause; the National Committee for Media and

Communication Reform; and the Independent High Commission for Elections.

- Components of civil society participated in all national dialogues organized after the elections of 23 October 2011, which were concerned with discussing the constitution bill, major national accord, political violence, and fighting terrorism.

- They also participated in preparing bills concerned with transitional justice and the national mechanism for preventing torture.

This important role, or roles, which the components of civil society in Tunisia have assumed, before and after 14 January 2011, should not obscure some essential elements that help us to understand this phenomenon on the one hand and to specify the components of civil society and their types, activities, methods of work, points of strength and weakness, and relationship between them on the other hand:

1. What characterizes civil society in Tunisia today is the significant number of associations, which has surpassed seventeen thousand registered associations in addition to syndicates, movements, groups, public figures, association media outlets, and activists such as bloggers. This great number makes it difficult for us to enumerate them, to specify their components, and to be able to categorize them later on.

2. The intertwinement of the components of civil society in Tunisia today between traditional and modern makes it somewhat difficult (even on the research level) to deal with these two kinds, as they do not possess the same elements, and they are not subject to the same standards.

3. Features of civil society in Tunisia have not yet been formed in a conclusive manner due to the transitional period the country is experiencing, which has had a great impact on all levels: political, juristic, economic, social, and also on the components of civil society. This explains the numerous and diverse forms of civil activity which we were not familiar with prior to 14 January, and which makes researching these components not subject to the same gauges.

4. The multiplicity and diversity of intertwined components in the public sphere after 14 January, led to the intertwinement of civil society activity and direct political activity. This makes it difficult to classify and determine the affiliation of some components as "civil society" or "political sphere" because some of them do not hide their proximity, affiliation, or allegiance to a certain political party.

5. Civil society activities vary according to their preset objectives; however, they intertwine occasionally in some associational activities. We can find that some traditional components of civil society and many modern components of this society practice numerous activities which are not necessarily consistent with their main objectives. This affects the classification of these components and the determination of their relationship with other components of civil society and political and public entities.

THE REALITY OF CIVIL SOCIETY

The reality of civil society in Tunisia today requires presenting the following preliminary notes:

1. The society scene today is characterized by the abundance and diversity of intertwined components: associations subject to the law of associations (more than seventeen thousand associations), associations subject to special legal texts, for example fishermen's associations and water associations (more than four thousand associations), organizations of active groups in cyberspace (hundreds), as well as influential national figures.

2. The existence of a great number of components of civil society prior to 14 January 2011 (more than ten thousand associations), and others which came about after that date and which are as numerous if not more so. This cohabitation requires us to determine the characteristics of civil society during transitional periods, especially so, since the features of this scene have not yet been conclusively set.

3. The civil society scene today is characterized by new forms of association and society work which did not exist in the same intensity and number prior to 14 January 2011. They are primarily represented in:
   - Youth movements, motions, and groups that are active virtually on the one hand and active in public spheres on the other. These are forms of unorganized work from a structural and legal standpoint, and not accustomed to the traditional forms of civil society work.
   - Religious associations, groups, and spheres that are heavily active, whether in the traditional form of civil society work (associations and unions like Al-Ai'mmah Union) or in unconventional forms of work: associations and groups that are active in mosques and online. There are no statistics concerning them despite their abundance and clear prevalence.

- Trade union pluralism and the formation of trade unions in sectors that were previously prohibited: the judiciary, security services, and customs.
- Inception of regularity for components of civil society within networks, whether on the national level or on the local and regional level; however, this phenomenon is still in its initial stages.

4. Intertwinement of the roles and functions between components of civil society, components of political society, and components of economic structures:
   - We notice the intertwinement of civil society and political society in one of two ways. The first is the convergence between political parties and the rest of the components of civil society, and the second is the convergence between these components and state agencies, which is notable in all movements organized by the ruling majority and the opposition.
   - As for the intertwinement of economic structures and civil society, we primarily notice it in regard to funding organizations and associations, which in turn, and in part, practice economic activities that are very close to the activities of economic structures.

5. The large number of organizations, bodies, and foreign and international centers in Tunisia and their influence on the society scene in Tunisia.

The diversity of the civil society scene in Tunisia requires that we handle and work on only their most important aspect (in number at least) which is the associations and, to be more specific, the associations subject to the law of associations and not those which were established based on special legal texts.

ASSOCIATIONS ARE AN ESSENTIAL COMPONENT OF TUNISIAN CIVIL SOCIETY

The Center of Media, Formation, Studies, and Documentations of Associations (IFEDA) data shows that the number of associations up to the beginning of July 2014 reached 17,245, of which, 7,245 associations were created after 14 January 2011. However, this number does not reflect the reality of the situation and does not mean that all these associations actually exist. It reflects the total number of associations that published the legal declaration for their formation in the official gazette i.e., there are associations that exist legally and there are those that exist in reality. It has not been possible to determine the number of associations that have disappeared or dissolved themselves.

Total Sum of Associations up to 1 July 2014

State	Science	Women	Sport	Cooperation	Culture & Art	Social Charity	Development	Childhood	Small Loans	School	Environment	Legal	Citizen	Youth	Network	Coordination	Total
Tunis	607	32	282	305	528	405	285	35	30	235	54	162	139	37	26	1	3163
Ariana	87	9	96	38	124	112	81	10	10	109	26	21	45	11	5	0	784
Ben Arous	47	2	93	25	125	95	40	11	12	126	17	11	18	18	3	0	646
Manouba	39	5	34	11	69	41	34	7	10	109	2	4	4	12	0	0	382
Nabeul	39	21	173	28	198	118	75	30	15	371	41	3	28	29	1	0	1172
Zaghwan	8	2	21	7	27	19	13	1	6	114	4	0	4	7	0	0	233
Bizerte	28	16	75	19	107	104	49	9	16	263	14	16	15	11	2	0	744
Beja	13	3	30	7	66	39	33	9	9	136	10	1	6	11	1	0	384
Jendouba	9	10	38	7	66	71	46	6	9	227	10	2	14	19	0	1	523
Kef	3	2	32	9	49	59	54	12	12	157	7	1	6	7	0	1	408
Silian	1	5	15	9	58	48	26	5	11	196	8	3	4	11	0	0	400
Kairouan	11	1	59	13	45	66	35	7	11	230	5	6	18	10	1	1	519
Kasserine	14	3	31	10	77	91	184	9	15	250	16	6	12	12	1	0	731
Sidi Bouzid	15	6	65	3	96	72	87	11	14	300	14	11	10	14	1	1	720
Sousse	60	1	55	39	166	113	58	17	17	189	18	5	30	17	1	2	788
Monastir	48	9	86	37	101	59	54	9	13	159	13	2	19	11	0	3	623
Mahdia	16	3	48	14	88	66	36	5	11	165	3	3	3	5	0	0	465
Sfax	130	8	137	121	256	153	67	32	16	488	21	13	22	32	0	0	1496
Gafsa	8	6	40	14	125	98	122	10	11	106	17	7	13	9	1	0	587
Tozeur	11	2	21	4	44	26	36	1	5	44	11	0	8	6	0	0	219
Tribal	6	10	35	9	94	68	48	8	8	115	9	5	6	3	0	0	424
Gabes	20	0	64	16	110	94	64	10	11	155	20	3	10	13	0	1	591
Medenine	24	6	59	11	131	128	88	16	8	277	20	3	22	15	1	1	810
Tataouine	7	5	29	11	96	66	48	8	8	121	4	5	13	10	1	1	433
Total	1251	167	1618	767	2846	2211	1663	280	288	4642	364	292	472	324	48	12	17245

www.ifeda.org.tn

53

Due to the large number of these associations, we must state the following preliminary notes regarding the methodology used in this research:

METHODOLOGY

DATA DOCUMENTATION AND ANALYSIS

This study of civil society in Tunisia followed the following steps:

DOCUMENTATION

Determining various documents concerned with civil society led to the adoption of the following studies and research papers:

Studies

- A study conducted in Arabic by the Arab Institute for Human Rights in June 2013. Its objective was to evaluate associations formed after 14 January 2014 through a representative sample that consisted of 128 associations, and to determine their characteristics, needs, and the challenges they face.
- A study conducted by Foundation For the Future (FFF) regarding Tunisian associations, which was published in French and English in April 2013.
- A study conducted in French by the European Union in June 2011, regarding Tunisian associations after the events of 14 January 2011.

Academic Research

Some scientific research (especially academic) was conducted that addressed some topics concerning civil society in general and Tunisian civil society in particular (a complete collection of these studies is listed in this study).

FIELDWORK

We based our fieldwork on a variety of methods in order to include various components of Tunisian civil society.

NUMBER OF PARTICIPANTS IN THIS STUDY

The number of participants reached 120 associations, vocational organizations, and trade unions. We conducted interviews with a number of people who participated in civil society work.

These participants are a large group that represents civil society. Care was taken in order for the sample to incorporate the following data:

- Balance in regional representation i.e., different regions in the country (the capital, the north east, north west, the middle, the coast, and the south). We selected the participants, who collaborated in different proportions, as follows:

REGIONAL REPRESENTATION

Tunis	25
The north east (Nabeul, Bizerte, and Kélibia)	35
The north west	11
The middle (Kairouan, Kasserine, and Sidi Bouzid)	16
Coastal region (Sousse and Mahdia)	8
The south (Sfax, Gabes, and Medenine)	25

- Balance between categories of associations: associations represented in this study include associations of human rights, sport and culture, development, charity, women's rights, child protection, special needs, trade unions, and media.
- Balance between gender of participants who were interviewed in person or on the phone.

TECHNIQUES USED IN FIELDWORK

We made an effort to diversify the techniques used:

The Questionnaire

The questionnaire included questions concerning the way the association presents itself. It included eleven questions surrounding: (1) the concept of civil society; (2) its components; (3) involving political parties in civil society; (4) public figures and civil society; (5) criteria of membership in civil society; (6) categories of components of civil society; (7) classification of associations; (8) points of strength of civil society; (9) challenges that civil society faces; (10) immediate needs of civil society; and (11) long term needs of civil society.

We sent the questionnaire to two hundred organizations, of which only fifty-five answered. They have different objectives and are from different ideological and intellectual currents and different geographical areas.

ORGANIZATIONS BY GEOGRAPHIC AREA

Nabeul	15
Tunis	14
Sfax	6
Mednin	6
Kaf	5
Kairouan	4
Benzart	2
Al-Qasreen	1
Qabes	1
Sidi Bou Zaid	1

Interviews: Two types were adopted:

- Direct interviews: We tried to film and record the greatest number possible; we were able to interview eleven civil society representatives. We were also able to interview officials in associations, vocational organizations, and unions (associations before 14 January 2011: the Association for Democratic Women, the Tunisian League for Human Rights, Amnesty International – Tunisia, the Association for Young Lawyers; and organizations after 14 January 2011: the Union for Judges, the Association for Judges,[1] the Union for Administrational Judges, and the Association for Tunisian Women).
- Phone interview: We made appointments with officials from forty associations with different objectives and from different locations. We conducted phone conversations with them.

A methodological guide was followed, which consisted of five main points: 1) Criteria for membership of civil society 2) Categories for the components of civil society 3) Points of strength of civil society 4) Challenges facing civil society 5) Immediate and long term needs of civil society.

Workgroups

In order to reach a result that encompasses most issues concerning civil society in Tunisia, we formed three workgroups. Each party consisted of seven participants from civil society organizations (i.e. twenty-one participants) from different regions, social classes, and affiliations.

USING THE RESULTS OF THE WORK

Despite working with a group that consisted of 120 participants, the diversity of the methods in use, and the diversity in the regional affiliation and categorization of the active parties, the study sample remains limited in comparison with the vast number of the components of civil society in Tunisia (over 17,000 associations). Therefore, the results of this work are mainly:

- An enrichment and analysis of all documents and results obtained.
- A clarification of the study's conclusions through concrete examples.
- To give the study a practical dimension.
- An enrichment of the study through fieldwork.
- To support the study through charts and tables.

ASSOCIATIONS IN TUNISIA

In this context, we will present the history of the formation of associations in Tunisia (I) and their legal regulation (II). We will then present the different categorizations through which regulators, or those interested in associational affairs, attempted to organize and encompass them (III). Finally, we will present a preliminary assessment of the status of associations in Tunisia at this point in time (IV).

I. HISTORY OF THE FORMATION OF ASSOCIATIONS IN TUNISIA

The association phenomenon in Tunisia witnessed two important booms, each of which was the result of an important political event. The first boom came after the political change that occurred on 7 November 1987 and continued for the following two years (1); the second boom followed the events of January 2011 (2).

THE FIRST ASSOCIATION BOOM 1988 – 1989

The first association boom lasted for two years following the political change on 7 November 1987. During these two years, 3,497 associations were formed i.e., 1,750 associations per year in comparison to an annual rate of seventy-five new associations in the period from 1980 to 1987.

This boom came as a result of the formation of a certain kind of association, known as associations for the development of elementary schools. In late December 2012, they numbered 4,622 associations; almost two-thirds of them were formed in 1988 and 1989. In 1988, 1,575 associations of this category were formed, which represented eighty-nine percent of the total associations formed that year. And in 1989, 1,439 associations were formed, which represented eighty-three percent of the total associations formed for that year. Therefore, the formation rate of associations not from this category did not exceed 156 associations per year (194 associations in 1988, and 119 associations in 1989). This warrants discussion, as it reveals itself as an artificial boom, which the former regime excessively exploited to polish its image and to give the illusion of qualitative change in the association scene in Tunisia.

The first boom clearly contradicts, in substance and essence, the current association boom that the country has been experiencing since 14 January 2011.

THE SECOND ASSOCIATION BOOM 2011 – 2013

The association scene after 14 January 2011 has been distinguished by the abundance of associations, which exceeded seventeen thousand in number as previously mentioned (7,245 were formed after 14 January). However, this abundance phenomenon is not, as it may seem at first sight, the most important feature of this stage. This change, although relative, as will be shown, is the direct result of the geographical diversity and distribution of these associations.

TOTAL NUMBER OF ASSOCIATIONS UP TO THE BEGINNING OF JULY 2014

Year	Number of Associations
2011	1975
2012	2286
2013	1668
2014 up to the beginning of July	916
Total up to the beginning of July	7245

When looking at the increase in the number of associations between 2011 and 2014, we can see the significant boom was restricted to 2011 and 2012 and started to slow down in 2013 and 2014 (the number of newly established associations reached 1,034 new associations at the end of 2014). This increase, especially between 2011, the year of national and political movement, and 2012 can be explained by the introduction of decree number eighty-eight on 24 September 2011 which governed existing associations. It facilitated the establishment of associations and, thus, 2012 witnessed the establishment of the greatest number of associations. The numbers started to slow down in 2013 and slowed down even more in 2014.

DIVERSITY

The current period is distinguished by the formation of associations in different fields including development, charity, human rights, environment, civil work, science, women's rights, and cooperation. However, this diversity is relative.

Aside from the entanglement of the fields in which these associations are active, many of them can be included in one category, which is associations specialized in human rights (environment associations, civil work associations, and women's rights associations) contrary to many specialized reports that separate them; even if we rely on this separation of association activities, the most important category remains the one which includes associations working in the field of human rights. This is a natural reaction to the former authoritarian regime. The importance of this category increases if we adopt a broad definition that squeezes in associations working in women's rights, environment, and other fields that are closely related to human rights.

In numbers, the following associations were formed after 14 January: two hundred human rights associations, 340 civil work associations (in contrast with eleven before 14 January), 180 environmental associations, sixty-eight women's rights associations, 1,100 cultural and artistic associations (20.4 percent of the total number of associations formed after 14 January) and 980 developmental associations (18.7 percent of the total number of associations formed after 14 January). This large number represents an important phenomenon compared to the phenomenon of charity associations, which are increasing in number and have reached 1,200 associations i.e., twenty-three percent of the associations formed after 14 January. Many of them show their ideological and religious affiliation and work within a set political course. It is worth noting a third important category which appeared due to the trade union pluralism that the country witnessed after 14 January and the expansion of the work of trade unions to include groups of employees who were legally forbidden from this practice under the former regime.

GEOGRAPHICAL DISTRIBUTION

The geographical distribution of associations differs according to regions and according to provinces in the regions. The province of the capital Tunis has the greatest number of associations (3,163 associations[2]), then comes Sfax (the second most important city after Tunis, 1,496 associations), after that Nabeul (one of the most important touristic cities in the north east, 1,172 associations).

The number of associations is less than a thousand in the remaining provinces, with the greatest number in Medenine (in the south east, 810 associations), and the provinces of the mid-west (Kairouan, Sidi Bouzid, and Kasserine), with a rate of six hundred associations for each province.

As for the north-west provinces (Beja, Jendouba, Kef, and Silian), the number of associations for each province is 420 associations.

During the time in which the association phenomenon was almost exclusive to major cities, especially the region of Greater Tunis, associations started to spread throughout the republic in provinces, most importantly those in the mid-east

(934 association in contrast to 1,898 in Greater Tunis), after that came the mid-west and the south west (524 associations in each area) and then the north east (432), then the south east (420), and the north west (265). However, this phenomenon must be put in its relative context, as the numbers reveal that the Tunis region leads in this field with 1,898 associations formed after 14 January 2011 i.e., thirty-eight percent of the total number of associations formed after the revolution. This region includes sixty-nine percent of the human rights associations that were formed after the revolution, sixty percent of scientific associations, forty-five percent of civil work and citizen associations, while one quarter of associations formed in the south are classified as charity associations. From a different standpoint, the geographical distribution feature regains its importance if we take into consideration the demographical weight of these associations in different areas. Based on this fact, we notice the dynamics in the mid-west and the south west in regard to association formation after 14 January which surpassed the mid-east. In the mid-west, one association was formed for every 2,099 people, in the south west, an association for 1,471 people, while in the mid-east, one association was formed for every 2,925 people. These numbers are close, especially those of the south west, to the rate of Greater Tunis, which is one association for every 1,358 people.[3] Delving deeper into geographical distribution, we find that a geographical difference in society numbers after 14 January 2014 can also be noticed between the capital of the province and inland areas. The capital of the province, in most cases, has more than half of the associations of the province (in Tetaouine it reaches sixty-seven percent), except for Nabeul where the city of Nabeul has thirty-five percent of existing associations in the province. This is contested by the cities of Kailbieh, Hamamat, Sulaiman, Gorba, and Grombalieh. This phenomenon can be explained by "cloning the centralist phenomenon that exists on the national level in favor of the province capital"[4] which usually enjoys the availability of infrastructure and the concentration of the elite. Numbers on record in Nabeul province support this explanation, as competing cities in this area do not lack the infrastructure present in the province capital.

BIPOLAR PHENOMENON

The political polarity based on ideology that characterizes the political arena clearly has a great influence on the association scene. It can be said that the association scene is divided between two parties: human rights associations that mostly rely on declared references on the one hand, and charity associations, with religious dimensions for the most part, on the other hand. This division occurs geographically as well. Civil society is in fact two societies which are almost separate geographically due to the clear numerical dominance of each category in certain areas. This is clarified by the aforementioned piece of information which states that one quarter of the formed associations in the south of the country fall into the category of charity associations and that sixty-nine percent of human rights associations formed after 14 January are focused in the Greater Tunis region.

Despite the adoption of the decree regulating associations issued on 24 September 2011, which opens the door to forming association networks, the number of these networks since that date has not exceeded forty-eight. Most of them are concentrated in the capital Tunis (twenty-six), then Ariana (which is close to the capital) (five), and there are three networks in Nabeul. As for the rest, the number of networks did not exceed one for each province; however, no networks were established in Zaghwan, Jendouba, Kef, or Silian (two, the north west), Sfax, Tribal, Tuzur, and Gabes in the south east and southwest. This shortage in forming networks is due to the novelty of this experiment and the lack of the associations' ability to act, manage, and deal with this concern, especially as most newly formed associations suffer greatly from difficulties in the management and governance level (which we will discuss later).

As for coordinates, it is no more than a name, as they are associations just like any other associations subject to this decree. Therefore, their very low number (twelve) is normal due to the lack of anything that distinguishes this "category." Coordinates are usually represented in a group of associations that is organized within a common framework, without being a network of association. In order for this framework to be more independent and receive adequate funding an association, called "the coordinate" is formed. Its board is formed by representatives of the associations that formed it i.e., associations form coordinates not to seek to increase the number of participants, but rather to increase the number of partner associations.

II. LEGAL REGULATIONS OF ASSOCIATIONS IN TUNISIA

The laws that have represented the legal framework regulating association activities in Tunisia for decades are law number 59-164, dated 7 November 1959,[5] revised in the basic law number 88-90, dated 2 August 1988, and the basic law number 92-25, dated 2 April 1990. However, the monitoring in place, which distinguished this legal system, made it entirely unsuitable for the movements after 14 January. Thus, the High Commission for Achieving the Goals of the Revolution, Political Reform, and Democratic Transition worked on establishing a new legal system in the freedoms sphere and sought to democratize public life. This effort gave fruit to the decree number 88-2011 of 24 September 2011[6] that annulled the law of 1959. Civil society representatives agree with the liberal spirit of this decree, enabling the activation and support for the engagement of associations in the democratization and development of the country.[7] This liberal spirit, which distinguishes the decree, is evident in its removal of different obstacles put in place by the 1959 law regarding association formation and reducing the limitations imposed on their management.

REMOVING OBSTACLES FACING FORMATION OF ASSOCIATIONS

In regard to the formation of associations, the decree of 2011 represented a huge step in comparison to the law of 1959 on many different levels.

PROCEDURES OF FORMATION

Establishing associations under the 1959 law from a legal standpoint used to be based on the media law, under the control of the minister of interior. He was authorized to declare his approval for forming an association or to reject its declaration according to a justified decision within a period not exceeding three months (often, justification was a formality). This procedure made associations subject to a licensing system, knowing that practicing any activity before obtaining the declaration or after the rejection of the declaration made the individuals concerned legally liable.

The decree of 2011 made establishing associations subject to the system of declaration (Chapter 10). At first glance, this may seem to be a continuity of 1959 law's objectives; however, the system was different in essence. Declaration in the new text is based on different procedures and produces legal consequences that are different from those of the 1959 law. According to the decree's requirements, the association must send a letter to the General Government Bureau, which replaced the Ministry of Interior. This represents an important alleviation from the administrational presence in the association sphere. After receiving notification of attainment, a representative of the association is charged with delivering an advertisement to the public press within seven days, which then must be published in the official gazette within fifteen days, starting from the day they delivered the advertisement. Not returning notification of attainment within thirty days of sending the letter is considered a notification (Chapter 11). The decree states that an association is considered legally established starting the day the letter was sent and gains its legal status starting from the date of publication of the advertisement in the official gazette (Chapter 12), contrary to the law of 1959 which stated "an association is not considered legally established and able to practice its activities until three months have passed starting the day the declaration is submitted." This gave the minister of interior room to "make a decision to refuse the formation of the association."

CATEGORIZING ASSOCIATIONS

The law of 1959 contained, as part of its monitoring obsession, a strict categorization of associations in its first chapter. It divided them into eight categories and limited their fields of work. This was cancelled by the decree of 2011, which does not present any categorization or any limitation on their fields of work. Based on its categorization mechanism, the law of 1959 did not allow associations "of public nature" to refuse any membership application or else they would be legally liable. This categorization was one of the methods used by the authorities to penetrate associations and enforce their monitoring upon them.

This was completely cancelled by the 2011 decree when it stated that "it is up to each society to determine its terms of membership" (Chapter 17).

DETERMINING AGE OF MEMBERS AND FOUNDERS

The decree of 2011 stated that associations can only be established by persons who are at least sixteen years of age. As for members, they must be at least thirteen years of age in contrast to the law of 1959 which did not specify any age limit either for the founders of the association or its members. The law of 1959 referred to civil law matters concerning the eligibility age, which was twenty years of age and had dropped to eighteen years by 1959. Therefore, persons under this age could not form associations or run for elections for their boards.

NATIONALITY OF MEMBERS AND FOUNDERS

The law of 1959 prohibited non-Tunisians from forming associations, which is clearly indicated in chapters sixteen and seventeen and implicitly acknowledged by requiring a national identity card from the founders as one of the prerequisites of the establishment dossier. The decree of 2011 opened the door to the possibility of Tunisia residents establishing associations on equal terms with those who hold Tunisian citizenship.

The liberal spirit of the decree is evident in its provisions for the formation of associations when compared with the requirements of the law of 1959; however, this does not prevent us from presenting some reservations concerning the decree of 2011. Perhaps the most important are the following three reservations.

1. The cancellation of the law of 1959 implicitly canceled the categorization of associations. This in and of itself is a positive step because it cuts off the jurisdiction of the administration in refusing the demand of declaration of associations based on its "decision" that they are not subject to legal categorization. However, this step also means the cancellation of the category of "associations of national interest," which were characterized by the nature of their fundraising, in addition to the necessity for depositing the funds of these associations in the name of the government or government organizations. Although the former regime used this category of associations as a means to seize public funds, there are many important associations in this category, like the Association for Protection from Road Accidents, Association of Tunisian Mothers, and The Tunisian Union for Solidarity. This raises the issue of the fate of these associations and the new approach that must be adopted in dealing with them in the decree of 2011.

2. The previous absence of a text concerning the age limit for founders of associations made this issue subject to civil law. However, the age limit of sixteen years in the decree of 2011 might pose legal problems. A sixteen year old young man might be

appointed head of an association, and at this age he is considered a minor and is not legally liable.

3. The decree of 2011 imposes on the founder of a foreign association delegation that they be residents of Tunisia; however, this status is usually not granted to concerned persons so long as the office of the association has not yet been established.

The notes above necessitate enhancing the decree through some practical texts to explain its requirements, uncover its ambiguity, and resolve anything that may seem contradictory in the text. However, it is true that this decree transferred the association system in Tunisia from lockout to liberalism and from maximum monitoring to effective freedom; this is what the decree has secured regarding association governance.

REDUCING OBSTACLES IMPOSED ON MANAGING ASSOCIATIONS

The decree of 2011 was able to reduce restrictions imposed on managing associations by annulling some of the requirements of the former legislation that tied up this freedom, and including issues that were absent from the law of 1959, which would support the freedom of managing associations and achieve transparency.

The changes that the decree brought about in regard to the legal management of associations were mainly concerned with the strict nature of the law of 1959.

REDUCING MONITORING OF ASSOCIATIONS

If an association did not abide by its legal requirements, the law of 1959 enabled the Ministry of Interior to temporarily close its headquarters and prohibit its members from meeting, even before a competent court issued a court ruling. The decree of 2011 prevents the administration from interfering in association affairs. In the case that associations do not abide by legal requirements, the decree states that the association is to continue its activities until a court ruling is issued to cease its activities or for it to be dissolved. The decree settles for this penalty, as it does not include any other penalties that deprive the liberties of the members of the association in contrast to the law of 1959, which included a prison penalty of up to one year, in the case of failing to abide by legal requirements. From a different standpoint, the decree endorsed the freedom of the association to change its bylaw by informing the General Government Bureau no later than one month from taking the decision (Chapter 16). This is a break off from the strictness of the 1958 law toward the freedom of associations to change their bylaws, and the resulting practices, like the Interior Ministry's habit in providing a ready-made bylaw (exemplary). The founders of the association merely filled in the boxes concerning the name of the association, its goals, names of the members, and headquarters, in addition to other matters that varied from one association to another; then they had it signed but were not able to change any of the requirements or the need, imposed by the 1959 law, on the part of the association to inform the administration about " a new division or branch or subdivision or a secondary group which is managed by or connected to it under a common system goal."

EXPANDING FREEDOMS OF ASSOCIATIONS

The decree supports freedom in association management and transparency. The legislators noticed the lack of legal requirements in the law of 1959 concerning certain matters in managing associations; a lack that was exploited by political authorities and their administrational apparatus in the former regime in order to weaken the associations' ability to work and to defend themselves in face of the authorities' attacks and tyrannical practices. Therefore, the decree fixed the loopholes by regulating association networking through its fourth chapter entitled "Association Networks."

According to the decree of 2011, two or more associations can establish a "network of association." This network gains an independent moral status on behalf of the associations that constitute it. The same legal system that regulates associations also regulates the formation and activities of networks. However, the addition that the decree of 2011 endorsed enabled associations to carry out activities in a common framework and establish binding associations while preserving the independence and the legal status of member associations, as this membership is for associations and not individuals.

ACCOUNTING AND FINANCIAL SPENDING OF ASSOCIATIONS

The decree of 2011 regulates all matters concerning financial spending and accounting for associations. It forces all associations that have resources that exceed one hundred thousand dinars to appoint an auditor (Chapter 43), in contrast to the law of 1959 which did not impose any requirements.

At the end of this quick presentation, it should be noted that certain requirements in the decree concerning managing associations pose practical problems, as many people concerned in association affairs point out,[8] for example, the issue of exemption of associations from VAT tax. This proves the point made earlier about the need for practical texts that facilitate their work and objectives.

MOST IMPORTANT DEVELOPMENTS OF THE ASSOCIATION LAW IN TUNISIA

	Law of 1959	Decree of 2011
Formation of Associations	• Informing the Minister of Interior • Need for a declaration • Minister of Interior has three months to declare the approval of the formation of the association • Association is not considered formed legally and does not have the right to practice any activity until three months have passed from the date the declaration was submitted	• Informing the General Government Bureau • Annulling the need for obtaining a declaration • Association is considered legally formed from date the letter was sent. It receives its legal status from the date of publication of the advertisement in the official gazette
	• The law prescribes eight categories for associations and limits their field of work • Associations with a "public nature" cannot refuse any request for membership or else they will be legally liable	• The decree does not state any categorization or any limitation on field of work. • It is up to each association to set its own terms for membership
	• The law does not state any age limit whether for the association's founders or its members	• Only persons who are at least sixteen years old can establish associations. As for members, they have to be at least thirteen years old.
	• Denies the right of non-Tunisians to form associations	• Tunisian citizens or residents can form associations
Governing Associations	• In case legal requirements are not respected, the Ministry of Interior can decide to temporarily close headquarters of the association and prohibit its members from meeting, even before a competent court issues a court ruling • The law provides for a penalty that deprives the freedom of the association's members and officials, which can be up to one year in prison	• The association continues its activities until a court ruling is issued for it to cease its activities or for it to be dissolved • The decree does provide for any penalties that deprive the freedom of the members of the association
	• Limited freedom for associations to change their bylaws	• Freedom for associations to change their bylaws by informing the General Government Bureau within one month of the decision
	• Absence of legal text concerning association networking	• Legal regulation of networking through "association networks"
	• Absence of legal text concerning associations rights in litigating	• Legal text concerning associations rights in litigating
	• Absence of requirements for accounting and financial spending	• Each association that has resources that exceed one hundred thousand dinars must appoint an auditor

III. Categorizing Associations

Associations can be categorized in different ways: there is a legal basis, a method adopted by some competent public institutions, or a method suggested by associations and organizations.

Legally Based Category

In this part, we present the contents of this category and go over its advantages and disadvantages before talking about the annulment of this category in the decree of 2011.

Contents of this Category and Advantages and Disadvantages

From a legal standpoint, we can talk about two categories for associations. One of them is included in the other. They are, as it is apparent from the requirements of the law of 1959, the general category on the one hand and, on the other hand, the "normal associations" category, which is itself a category within the general category.

According to the general categorization, associations are classified into three categories.

Normal Associations

This category includes eight categories, according to law number 25 in 1999 which is a revision of the law of 1959:

- Women's rights associations
- Sport associations
- Scientific associations
- Cultural and artistic associations
- Charity, emergency, and social associations
- Developmental associations
- Cooperation associations
- Associations of a public nature

Associations of National Interest

To obtain this status, an association had to submit an application at least two years after its formation. It was then granted this status according to a decision by the interior minister. This status could be withdrawn from any association that violated its legal obligations or the regulations of its statute. Regulations for these associations are in Chapters 12 to 15 in the law of 1959. Important associations like National Union for the Blind, National Union for Women, and Tunisian Union for Solidarity and others enjoyed the privileges granted for the category. Privileges were mainly concerned with raising money, in addition to the ability to deposit funds in government stocks or government institutions (treasury bonds for example).

Foreign Associations

Foreign associations are defined in Chapter 16 in the law of 1959 as organizations that have the same characteristics as associations, and that have headquarters abroad or in Tunisia. They are governed by an administrational commission where at least half of the members are foreigners. According to the law of 1959, these associations could not be formed or practice any activity in Tunisia until the interior minister had signed their statute after consultation with the foreign minister. This signature was given on a temporary basis, could need to be regularly renewed, or could be withdrawn at any time based on a decision from the interior minister. An association's non-compliance with legal regulations could result in dissolving the association and annulling its work; this annulment was endorsed by a decision from the interior minister and resulted in the liquidation of the association's assets.

In order to distinguish between foreign associations and non-governmental organizations, the legislator singled out the latter in the statute number eighty for 1993, dated 26 July 1993, concerning establishment of NGOs in Tunisia. This law defined NGOs as associations, groups, and organizations that do not seek profit regardless of their form, nature, or objectives for which they were formed, and whose administrators and members belong to more than one country and practice their activities on a global or regional level. This law enables NGOs to own assets and property required for their activity and dispose of them, accept grants, donations, and aid, and litigate in courts. These organizations also enjoy exemption from taxes, fees, and custom taxes on equipment, vehicles, and products that must be owned or imported for them to practice their activity.

The question of the goal behind this dual categorization must be raised.

It is notable that resorting to this legal classification sought to limit the freedom of management for one category of associations, the associations of public nature, by imposing restrictions. This opinion is supported by the absence of the category of human rights associations which were categorized as associations of public nature and thus, they were subject to the restrictions imposed on this category. The Tunisian League for the Defense of Human Rights has suffered from the consequences of this categorization. It took this suffering to the administrational court against the Ministry of Interior. As a reaction to this unjust legislative reality, the decree of 2011 explicitly annulled the law of 1959, which was revised by the laws of 1988 and 1990; it also annulled the law of 1993.

THE DECREE OF 2011's ANNULMENT OF THE LAW OF 1959's CATEGORIZATION

The decree of 2011 explicitly annulled the law of 1959 and refrained from specifying any categorization for associations. All experts agree that this decree annulled the legal categorization of associations. However, the question remains surrounding the extent and scope of this annulment. Did this decree annul the general categorization of associations (normal associations, associations of public nature, foreign associations) or did it only annul the categorization of normal associations?

The relevance of this questions stems from three factors:

1. There is no categorization in the text of the decree except for national and foreign associations.
2. There is no category for associations of national interest in the text of the decree, which is one of its drawbacks.
3. The problem that foreign associations pose under the decree of 2011, which states that it "annuls the statute number eighty of 1993, dated 26 July 1993, concerning establishment of NGOs in Tunisia," is that annulment created a vacuum in regard to provisions regulating them. Does the decree consider these associations enlisted in the foreign association category which are regulated in its third part (Chapters 20 to 25)? The answer to this question is not evident, especially since the decree defines foreign associations as "a branch of an association established according to the laws of a different country" (page twenty of the decree), which seems incompatible with the status of NGOs as international legal entities.

In general, the answer to this issue tends to be:

1. The decree completely annulled the category of normal association without any room for doubt.
2. Ignoring the category of associations of national interest leads to two things:
   - Either the decree, which explicitly annulled the law of 1959 containing this categorization, has consequently annulled associations of national interest. This conclusion raises problems in dealing with associations in this category and requires a way of regulating them in a new text
   - Or the decree omitted them, which leaves them in a legal vacuum. In this case, the legislator can re-regulate them in a new text without posing any problems with regard to the decree of 2011.

3. The decree maintained the distinction between national and foreign associations. However, the question remains as to whether NGOs are categorized as foreign associations according to this decree or not. If the answer to this question is "no" then there is a need to regulate NGOs in a special text since the decree annulled the law of 1993 that was concerned in this matter. I tend to consider that the decree annulled this distinction between foreign associations and NGOs and that the latter is therefore enlisted as a foreign association, which is supported by the decree's usage of general words in defining foreign associations.

CATEGORIZATION MENTIONED ON THE IFEDA[9] WEBSITE

The Center of Media, Formation, Studies, and Documentation of Associations (IFEDA) categorizes associations into fourteen categories according to their activities and objectives. They are:

- Citizenship associations
- School associations
- Small loans associations
- Environment associations
- Development associations
- Cultural and artistic associations
- Charity, social, and emergency associations
- Human rights associations
- Sport associations
- Youth associations
- Science associations
- Cooperation associations
- Women's rights associations
- Childhood associations

What distinguishes this categorization is that:

1. It relies on a clear standard that does not interfere with other standards as is the case with legal categorization.
2. The association scene can be read more clearly.
3. It reveals association categories that the legal categorization previously obscured by including them in the associations of public nature category.

However, it suffers from a few shortages. Perhaps the most important are:

1. Not depending on internal categorization required by categories such as human rights associations.
2. Distinguishing between categories that could have been listed within one category, such as environment associations, citizenship organizations, and childhood organizations, which could have been placed within human rights organizations. This criticism remains relative if we take into consideration the particularity of each association's activities.

This consideration justifies separating these associations from the category of human rights associations; however, it could have been possible to show the particularity of these associations' activities through adopting subcategories within the category of human rights associations.

CATEGORIZATION ADOPTED BY ORGANIZATIONS THAT STUDY ASSOCIATIONS IN TUNISIA

Some organizations that worked on the association phenomenon in Tunisia resorted to a categorization based on the objectives of the association and its field of activity, including a categorization mentioned in a study conducted by the Future Foundation, dated 13 January 2013, which is very close to the categorization mentioned in IFEDA website. However, it singles out associations working in small loans in their own special category. This mandates the same precautions mentioned previously regarding IFEDA's categorization. Perhaps these precautions are more relevant in regard to this study, which was carried out after 14 January and emphasized the need to take into consideration the changes in the association scene after that date, without affecting the categorization it adopts afterwards.

The dominant feature of the work of these organizations is that it does not present a clear, broad definition, but rather, it settles for presenting a sub-categorization for these associations, taking into consideration their interest in, and focus on human rights associations, which is in line with the current situation. The categorization that the Euro-Mediterranean Network for Human Rights[10] suggests subdividing human rights associations into associations concerned in civil and political rights, associations that work in economic, social, and cultural rights, associations that work in the field of solidarity rights, associations concerned in women's rights, and associations of faction rights (children, the elderly, the handicapped). The benefit that ought to be obtained from the interlaced reading of these different categorizations is a dual benefit:

First–The need to find a general categorization which reflects the particularity of the current situation, as associations working on democratic transition issues can be placed in a special category, or they can be given a special category within human rights associations, which leads us to the second benefit.

Second–The need to suggest subcategories for human rights associations. This sub-categorization of human rights associations may include categories mentioned in the general categorization, in addition to new categories which can be adapted to the particularity of the association scene in Tunisia after 14 January, without neglecting the classical categorization based primarily on generations of human rights, which was adopted by the Euro-Mediterranean Network for Human Rights, as previously noted.

IV. EVALUATING THE STATUS OF ASSOCIATIONS IN TUNISIA

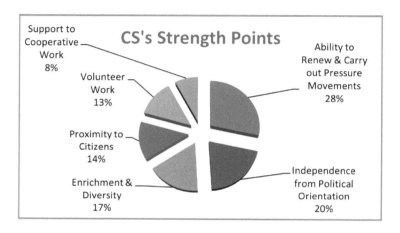

Civil
society in Tunisia after 14 January is marked by its active presence in the public scene and its influence on social movements. It is no longer a democratic display to polish the image of the regime. This gave it many features including spontaneity, independence, and struggle.[11]

The following chart may clarify the development that civil society witnessed after 14 January, where the ability to renew and carry out pressure movements occupies an important percentage within the framework of association activity. It is one of the most prominent points of the strength of associations (twenty-nine percent), after that comes independence from political orientation (twenty-one percent); this element is very important especially after a period in which civil society witnessed a state of loyalty and submission to the requirements and fantasies of the former political regime. Enrichment and diversity, proximity to citizens, and volunteer work come next. We find that the lowest percentage is for cooperative work which represents only eight percent of the points of strength of civil society.

Although these features concern civil society in general, they cast their shadow on associations, though on a minor level in many cases. Anyone evaluating the status of associations in Tunisia faces many obstacles. The most important of which are:

- Abundance – which prevents a comprehensive study of all the associations established in the Tunisian scene.
- Diversity – which is a historical diversity: old associations that were established under the former regime, and new associations that were formed after the revolution of 14 January. Old associations are divided into associations that have mingled into the social fabric of the country and reflect the aspirations of the individuals of the society, and associations that served the regime and its figures' interests. They reacted to the events of 14 January in different manners; some of them stopped their activities, while others are trying to take their position once again in the scene.
- Diversity in size and ability to influence–based on this, we can distinguish between effective and strong associations and associations which are still in the embryonic phase. This diversity in size and ability to influence entails a diversity in the geographical distribution of associations, which is no less influential on their presence in the association scene.

Therefore, all the reports that have been prepared or may be prepared remain incapable of giving a precise image or drawing up fixed and general characteristics for all components of the association fabric in the country, which makes their findings relative and their results mere indicators for the status of associations in Tunisia. The reality of associations in Tunisia after 14 January drives us to track their points of strength and weakness, whether on the level of

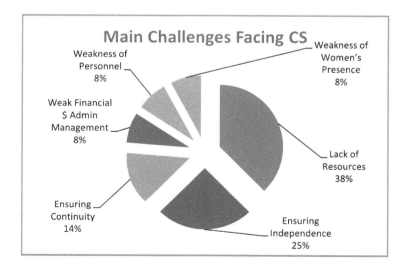

self-capability of the associations or on the level of their place in the public sphere.

ASSOCIATION CAPABILITY

From the above chart, it is clear that the lack of resources is on the top of the list of challenges that impede the work of associations with a percentage of thirty-eight percent. This explains the second impediment, no less important than the first, which is ensuring independence, estimated at twenty-five percent. In third place comes ensuring continuity, with a percentage of fourteen percent. The weakness of financial and administrative management, weakness of personnel, and weakness of women's presence are also impediments, but they come in fourth place with a percentage of eight percent.

The capability indicator is concerned with the status of the association itself i.e., measuring its internal potential and relies on five characteristics:

First – Governance – which is measured through:

- Engagement in action (an association's possession of referents other than its statute, like short-, mid-, or long-term plans that are prepared in a collective and participatory manner – an association's organization of periodical meetings and preparation of the minutes of these meetings).
- Transparency in management (allocating tasks clearly inside the association – preparing a financial report supported by accounting documents and available to different partners).
- Independence in making decisions (relationship between members of the association and political parties – the extent of the effect of joint work with political parties on the association's independence – decision-making in a collective and participatory manner that allows all members to express their aspirations).

Second – Human Resources – measured by the association's ability in:

- Personnel mobilization (extent of women's presence – relying on volunteers or on employees – members' expertise in association fieldwork – the association's ability to arouse the interest of its members in association work such as enabling them to participate in workshops, trips, and travel).
- Adequate personnel training in fields related to the association's work, managing projects, administrational work, and communication.

Third – Financial Resources – measured by:

74

- Ability to secure these resources (self securing – plurality of methods to find funds – extent of knowledge of potential funding – submitting serious funding requests – ability to communicate and negotiate).
- Financial independence (the association's financial resources: subscriptions – member donations – special donations – public donations – foreign donations – one financier or more – the association's ability to impose its decisions in its relationship with funding parties).

Fourth – Communication Capability – measured by:

- Ability to network (Does the association work within a network? Does it belong to a network? Does it belong to a network and has it completed a project within it? Does it seek to develop its networking capabilities?).
- The association's relations with the media and public mood (the association seeks, in a permanent and serious manner, cooperation with the media of different orientations – the association seeks to influence decision makers).

Fifth – Operational Capacity of the Association – it can be measured by:

- Efficacy of planning and execution of projects (the presence of a project calendar prepared in a collective and participatory manner – setting aside a specific budget for each project; the association works on abiding by it and paying for the services provided).
- Effect of the association's work on targeted people (the association relies on evaluation and following up on its projects, and uses that to influence decision makers – the association observes the opinions of those who are interested in its activities and those whom it targets, and takes advantage of that in its future work).

Based on these criteria, the internal capability indicator, as presented through the following elements, seems negative in Tunisia:

AGE GROUPS OF MEMBERS OF ADMINISTRATIONAL COMMISSION

This chart for the members of the administrational commission shows a weakness in the representation of the under-thirty-five-year-old sector. It varies between eighteen percent in Kef province and thirty-five percent in Medenine and Nabeul provinces. The thirty-five-to-sixty-year-old age group dominates the management of associations and it reaches its top percentage in Kef with seventy-nine percent and lowest in Sfax and Nabeul. We also notice a weakness in the above-sixty-year-old sector i.e., the sector that has retired; this sector has an effective presence in association work in developed countries.

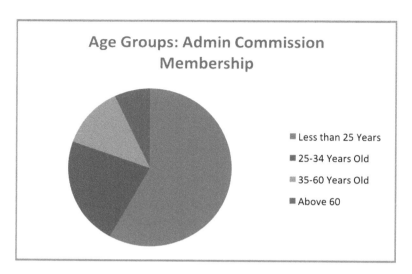

Age Groups: Admin Commission Membership

- Less than 25 Years
- 25-34 Years Old
- 35-60 Years Old
- Above 60

PERSONNEL DISTRIBUTION ACCORDING TO GENDER

Concerning personnel distribution according to gender, it must be noted that women's presence is a little over one third. However, if we view the geographical distribution, we will notice a big difference in women's presence throughout provinces. In northern provinces, it almost reaches one half (forty-eight percent in Tunis, forty-seven in Nabeul), whereas the percentage of women declines below one third in other provinces (Sfax thirty-one percent, Kef thirty percent, Medenine twenty-four percent).

PERSONNEL DISTRIBUTION ACCORDING TO AGE GROUPS

The youth and elderly are evenly distributed; however, the elderly are dominant in management, something which we also find in the structure of political parties where the youth basis of the personnel is relatively broad and becomes narrower in management.

ASSOCIATIONS' SCOPE OF WORK

An inspection of the associations' scope of work indicates the dominance of national character on the work of associations that were included in the field research. Associations with a scope of work that reaches a national level represent more than fifty-four percent. This can be explained by the large number of associations that belong to the province of Tunis and which represent thirty-six percent (these association have great financial and human capabilities, which enable them to work on the national level). On the other hand, it can be explained through the nature of their fields of intervention, such as the social,

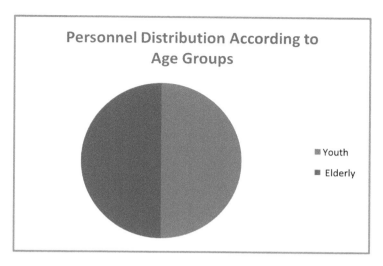

Personnel Distribution According to Age Groups

- Youth
- Elderly

economic, human rights,   a n d
transparency fields. These fields lead many associations to seek to come up with programs of actions that are not limited to the regional level, but rather seek to open up to the national level. In second place, we find that one quarter of associations in this study are active solely on a local level; this percentage increases outside the capital. While this phenomenon may seem logical for associations that are located outside capitals of provinces, it indicates when it comes to associations whose headquarters are in the capital of the province that there may be a kind of retraction of the elite towards their cities. Associations with a regional dimension come in last place with twenty percent of associations in this study. It must be noted that associations' declarations of their regional radiance does not necessarily mean that their activities cover the entire province, but rather it means that they may go beyond the local level, according to its narrow definition of activity in only one part of the region.

DIVERSITY OF ACTIVITIES OF "MERITING" ASSOCIATIONS

Diversity in activities stands out as a feature that makes us distinguish between associations. However, after questioning the associations in this study, we found that certain activities dominate.

Organizing Symposiums and Structural Training Sessions

More than half of the associations organize scientific and intellectual symposiums over various time periods. They might focus on one aspect (elections, for example), or there may be a diversity of aspects (transitional justice, individual freedoms, environmental problems, writing the constitution, etc.). Thirty percent of them organize structural training sessions that host different numbers of participants (this may reach thousands in election observation, and may not exceed a few individuals in transparency). Some of the managers at the participating associations indicated that funding is focused on the issue of structure, and considered this an exaggeration of some sort. They also believed that using part of the money allocated for structure towards establishing productive projects would have a bigger effect and better feasibility, especially since many structural training sessions are highly expensive given the fact that they rely on foreign experts, who are highly paid, in addition to the fact that some of the mentioned sessions are held in luxurious and expensive locations. The structural process may not include a large number of beneficiaries; some of the managers at the associations in question stated that some cadres at the associations monopolize a great number of structural training sessions (for recreational purposes rather than scientific benefit because of the repetition factor), and that some of those participants are older in age, rather than the youth group targeted by these sessions.

Organizing Awareness Campaigns

About twenty-nine percent of the associations in question organized awareness campaigns directly related to their activities. For example, associations active in elections organized awareness campaigns on the occasion of the elections of the National Constituent Assembly to urge citizens, especially the youth and women, to register in electoral lists, and in a later stage they invited them to participate in voting.

Distribution of Donations

More than one official in the associations in question declared that, among the other activities they carried out, more than twenty-six percent of associations distributed donations to those in need. What is striking in this regard is that only sixteen percent of the 120 associations we studied are charity, emergency, and social associations, and we must take into consideration that some associations that belong to this category do not actually carry out this activity. Therefore, it must be stated that many associations that belong to other categories (some of them are development associations, others are of public nature or women's rights associations) carry out the role of distributing donations to those in need. Ostensibly, this does not fit their stated objectives and categorization, which raises questions surrounding the reasons and settings that may explain this choice. It may be a spontaneous matter that is not subject to certain agendas, or it may be circumstantial i.e., related to an exceptional situation (like the exceptional snow fall or floods that the north-west part of Tunisia witnessed in 2012). In this regard, it must be noted that more than thirteen percent of the associations in question declare that they have organized relief and aid convoys in the context of the association's members' pursuit to guarantee some outreach for their organization in certain social sectors.

Field Interventions

Making an inventory of other important activities carried out by the associations in question reveals that a large percentage of these organizations (forty percent) performed field interventions related to their activity. Some officials in development associations or associations of public nature intervene in environmental issues either to preserve marine life, to spread the culture of citizenship and solidarity, or to avoid negligence on the part of special prosecutions that manage Tunisian municipalities in the transitional period. These officials revealed the associations' contributions in cleaning and forestation campaigns. Some development associations or charity, emergency, and social associations have completed or funded maintenance work for buildings affiliated with educational institutions or for needy citizens who lived in inadequate homes. In reality, we observe a great diversity in the scope of field interventions.

Organizing Cultural and Artistic Events

Although the associations in question that are categorized as cultural and artistic do not exceed 5.5 percent, the percentage of associations that stated that they organized cultural and artistic events is almost nineteen percent, including events that targeted a specific audience like children or student youth, or individuals with special needs. Others were aimed at the general public: people living in a certain area or even visitors of this area. Many associations combine holding cultural and artistic events with organizing recreational activities; about fifteen percent of associations carry this out. This may fall within charity activity when it targets certain groups such as orphans, or cultural activity if it is manifested in a form of a museum trip or a trip to archaeological sites.

Supporting Economic Projects

More than sixteen percent of the associations in question, especially those categorized as development associations, have turned to supporting economic projects, either by providing practical ideas for the targeted group or by supporting it financially through part of the infrastructure, facilities, or funds.

Participation in Making Regional or Local Administrational Decisions

There are various forms of association intervention in public affairs. What catches our attention in this context is that twelve percent of the associations in question acknowledged participating in making regional or local administrational decisions by attending consultations and meetings, and exercising pressure. This is the practice of advanced local democracy mechanisms; it includes regional or local administrational decisions, which the local association fabric helps to crystallize, and which represent the foundation for development.

Exercising Pressure on the National Constituent Assembly

Some associations that are active on the national level have stated that they have exercised pressure on the National Constituent Assembly, as part of their interest in public affairs, to assert some articles of the constitution such as those mentioned in "Tunisia's Oath for Freedom," or to modify some articles, especially those that contradict the civil status of the state. Other associations in question, especially those active in elections, took it upon themselves to monitor and exercise media pressure on some of the legislative acts of the National Constituent Assembly, especially drafting the law concerning the Independent Higher Commission for Elections, and choosing the members of the aforementioned commission. In this same context, we were able to observe six out of 120 of the associations in question, which played the role of a mediator in order to preserve social peace during local or regional conflicts. This decreases the level of violence and avoids resorting to security solutions that have been proven to be sterile in many instances. It also gives the association fabric moral authority that forces the regional or local administrational authority to consult with it and comply with its points of view in matters of public interest.

Listening Cells for Communicating with Victims

Among the activities with limited presence, it can be indicated that some the associations in question (three percent) created listening cells for communication with victims of human rights violations by public authorities or society. Other associations stated that they are determined to take it upon themselves to carry out this kind of activity within their future plans because of the immense psychological benefits it has for victims and its great importance in diagnosing social problems.

Publications and Releases

We notice an obvious weakness in publications and releases; fifty-three percent of the associations in question state that they publish and distribute paper publications, but in seventy-six percent of the cases these are just brochures about the association of an awareness nature. Associations that have published at least one book constitute less than fifteen percent, while less than four percent state they have published periodicals. As for associations that stated that they have published digital publications, their percentage is limited (less than fifteen percent). This is due to the absence of a dedicated website for the association or even a page on social networks. It could also be due to not committing to updating when the content is very limited or not updated at all because of the lack of financial or human resources, or as a result of insufficient interest in media in the association's activity.

MATERIAL FRAME FOR THE WORK OF THE ASSOCIATIONS IN QUESTION: HEADQUARTERS

The study focused on three issues concerning the material frame for the work of the associations in question. This first was the legal status of the place i.e., the headquarters in which the association operates. The second was the specifications of the aforementioned place (size and condition). The third was the suitability of the available equipment at the place in which the association operates.

LEGAL STATUS FOR THE HEADQUARTERS IN WHICH THE ASSOCIATION OPERATES

We were able to note, concerning the legal status for the place in which the association operates, that about one third of the associations in question lease the place they use as a headquarters, and more than one fifth of associations (twenty-two percent) use a place provided by a private or public party, and one fifth of associations (twenty percent) use headquarters provided by one of the association managers or personnel. Field research has shown that twenty-one out of 120 associations (sixteen percent) do not have headquarters, which leads to the cessation of the association's activities or to the necessity on part of its members to meet in cafés or at some of their homes and to carry out activities in public spheres or at the headquarters provided by other associations on the day of the activity. Some associations were able to obtain headquarters by virtue of the situation created by the changes that followed 14 January 2011, whereby many associations took over organizations affiliated with the former regime, especially the headquarters of the Constitutional Democratic Rally Party, and more than six percent of associations use this kind of headquarters by imposing a fait accompli. This percentage was higher in 2011; however, some municipalities, like the municipality of Meidoon in Jarba Island, reached a legal settlement for these places. It took over the former headquarter of Al-Tajammo' University in Meidoon, which had been taken over by some associations after 14 January 2011, but, at the same time, it converted the building into a housing for associations and signed leases with symbolic fees for these associations. The research revealed one unique case of an association that is active in headquarters that it owns; this constitutes less than one percent of the study sample.

SPECIFICATIONS OF THE HEADQUARTERS IN WHICH THE ASSOCIATION OPERATES

More than two thirds of association managers (sixty-eight percent) stated that the specifications of the headquarters in which their association operates are suitable for their activities; the remaining third considered that the headquarters do not possess the required specifications.

The third issue in regard to the material frame for the work of the associations in question is concerned with the suitability of available equipment at the place in which the association operates. What we mean by this is office and communication equipment (desks, cabinets, computers, printers, copy machines, telephones, fax machines, and internet subscription). Other equipment may be added like big tables, a large number of chairs, projectors, and display screens, etc. About forty-six percent of those asked stated that their headquarters are suitable for activities, whereas a third (thirty-two percent) considered them weak to the extent that they hinder activities, and twenty-two percent considered that the available equipment at the association headquarters does not help carrying out activities in a suitable manner. This means that more than one half of

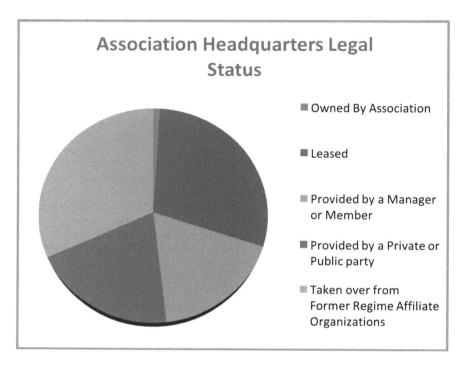

Association Headquarters Legal Status

- Owned By Association
- Leased
- Provided by a Manager or Member
- Provided by a Private or Public party
- Taken over from Former Regime Affiliate Organizations

associations have equipment that is below average according to their standards, which results in structural fragility. It must be noted that we did not include associations without headquarters (sixteen percent) in the calculations of these percentages.

PRESENCE OF SALARIED WORKERS WITHIN THE STRUCTURE OF THE ASSOCIATION

It is noticeable that two thirds of the associations in question rely solely on volunteers, whereas the other one third relies on salaried workers, whose numbers vary from one association to another, in addition to chief managers who are volunteers. Most associations rely on salaried workers classified as implementation helpers (guard duty, cleaning, secretaries etc.), whereas a minority rely on cadres that execute plans such as executive managers and project coordinators. It must be noted that some of the associations in question benefited from public procedures for youth employment when they hired salaried workers, especially those directed at holders of postgraduate degrees, and the overall wage which the young man/woman receives may come solely from the public procedures for employment. In this field research, we were not able to grasp the standards adopted by the public authorities to grant or decline

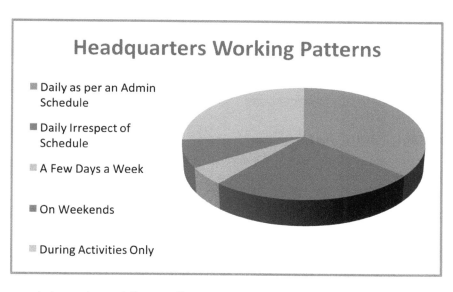

Headquarters Working Patterns

- Daily as per an Admin Schedule
- Daily Irrespect of Schedule
- A Few Days a Week
- On Weekends
- During Activities Only

associations the privileges of
youth services that are enlisted in programs adopted by the public procedures for employment, as we noticed that there are some civil societies that need this sort of support but do not enjoy it.

During the interviews, we asked some association managers about their vision of what professionalism should be like in the association scene. A few answered that there is no place for professionalism in the association field considering that, according to them, it contradicts the philosophy of real association work, which is based on volunteering. On the other hand, most of those asked saw that associations should incorporate a dose of professionalism to ensure the sustainability of these organizations' activities and the effectiveness of some of their interventions, but on the condition that decision-making authority remains in the hands of volunteers or elected members because this is the guarantee for preserving the identity of the organization.

THE ASSOCIATION'S RATE OF WORK IN ITS HEADQUARTERS

Addressing the issue of the association's rate of work in its headquarters, i.e., the frequency of opening up the headquarters, falls into the context of measuring the vitality of associations and their material presence in their social surrounding. Results have shown a correlation between the regularity of opening the association headquarters and the presence of salaried workers within the human resources of the association. The results show that in the majority of associations (thirty-six percent) where the managers stated that they have a daily rate of opening according to an administrative schedule, most have stated that they rely on salaried workers in administrational work for the association.

Whereas, one quarter of associations (twenty-five percent) open their headquarters on a daily basis without respect for an administrative schedule, but rather whenever the circumstances of the managers allow for that to happen. This is usually the case after they have fulfilled their professional commitment. A little more than a quarter of the associations have stated that the opening up of their headquarters is occasional, and only occurs on the occasion of activities (twenty-six percent).

FUNDING AND DONOR INITIATIVES

Since 14 January 2011 we have noticed the increased interest of donors and financiers in Tunisian association activities, especially those recently formed. However, we and the participating associations have witnessed that this mounting role for donors and financiers has gone through two stages:

- The first stage corresponded with the first year of the fall of the dictatorship. It continued until after the elections of 23 October 2011 (almost until mid-2012). It was distinguished by important funding for association activities without regulation by funding strategies on the part of the donors; the impression was that donors dedicated large sums of money that must be spent in a certain time, which led to the funding of similar projects and even identical projects without any coordination.
- The second stage started in mid-2012 and continues to this day. It is distinguished by increasing clarity in donors' work and choosing associations that are in financial crisis because most of these associations did not have a work strategy, funding sustainability, or a developing trust relationship with donors.

These primary elements for approaching funding must not mask the very important issues in funding associations in Tunisia, especially the new ones:

What happened in Tunisia, when the dictatorship collapsed, led to the flocking of donors to the country, but also led them to face their responsibilities to review their interactions with associations, because before 14 January 2011, donors were not allowed to deal freely with associations. With the collapse of the regime, donors had to expand in regard to the number of associations they fund and the type of activities and programs funded, and also the geographical distribution of these associations.

Regarding the number of associations that enjoyed funding from donors, we notice that most of the present associations have enjoyed direct or indirect funding (all associations participating in this study benefited at least once from funding).

In regard to projects and activities, donor parties expanded in order to fund activities and projects that were banned before 14 January 2011, especially in the fields of civil and political rights, or activities that can be grouped under "citizenship projects." In this framework, most associations (all associations participating in this study) developed projects that enlisted citizenship elements.

In regard to the number of donors, we witnessed a remarkable development especially after 14 January 2011, with the arrival of new donors who would not have been active in Tunisia before that date. In addition to traditional donors (United Nations programs, the European Union, some foreign cooperation agencies especially from France and Germany, and some German institutions that are active in Tunisia), we notice the arrival of new donors especially the Open Society Foundation (OSF) and foreign embassies in Tunisia: the Netherlands, Denmark, the United Kingdom, Sweden, Finland, and Switzerland.

This plurality in the number of donors also led to the designation of large sums of money for associations.

It is noticeable that most financiers and donors increased their support for associations two fold and three fold, and even four fold in some cases after 14 January.

The European Union, for example, designated fourteen million dinars (about eight million dollars) to support civil society in the period 2011-2014. As for the United Nations Development Program, it designated ten million dinars for the same period. Money designated by foreign cooperation (Spain, Switzerland, Finland, and France) exceeded a million dinars (refer to the study conducted by the Future Foundation surrounding civil society organizations in Tunisia, 2013, pp. 59).

SUMS OF MONEY DESIGNATED FOR SUPPORTING CIVIL SOCIETY IN TUNISIA

Financiers	Sums of Money Designated for Supporting Civil Society (in Tunisian Dinars)
European Union	14 million (2011-2014)
United Nations Development Program	10 million (2011-2014)
Swiss cooperation	1.6 million (2011-2012)
Spanish cooperation	1.6 million (2011-2013)
Finnish Embassy	1.5 million (2011-2013)
African Development Bank	1.2 million (2012)
Institute of French Cooperation	1 million (2011-2012)

Euro-Mediterranean Network for Human Rights	0.5 million (2011-2012)

This first stage, which was dominated by a quantitative character, settled down and started to recede in favor of a more rational stage. It was notable that associations, especially the new ones, were incapable of properly handling their resources and rules of governance, especially as they were not accustomed, formed, or trained for this.

This observation led to donors supporting and designating money to support associations' capabilities and train them in structural, administrational, financial and behavior, and to prepare projects and organize activities.

This motivated a group of financiers to form a "coordination team between financiers and international organizations." This initiative, which was put forward by the European Union, resulted in creating the Matrix of Projects as a summary of the most important projects that have been planned or are still being planned. This table included, up to September 2012, 162 projects to support civil society in Tunisia. It included seven countries and three international organizations: the United States of America (forty-eight projects), the European Union (twenty-four projects), the United Kingdom (eighteen projects), Spain (twenty-two projects), France (ten projects), the Netherlands (nine projects), Germany (eight projects), Food and Agriculture Organization (four projects), Japan (four projects), and the United Nations Development Program (two projects).[12]

This coordinated work between different intertwined parties led to better organization of funding and better definition of goals and projects. It enabled financiers to better identify associations which are capable of administering and sustaining projects.

FUNDING ASSOCIATIONS

We inquired about the funding sources of associations and were surprised at the lack of reservation surrounding this sensitive topic, which is rarely revealed automatically by documents related to this topic.[13]

Self-Funding

Generally speaking, eighty percent of the associations' resources come from membership fees. This number does not raise questions, although it is high; however, the remaining twenty-percent may be subject to question, especially as the percentage of associations that were questioned and inactive is a lot less than the latter percentage. Many association mangers do not want or are not capable of collecting membership fees, which weakens the relation between the association and some of the beneficiaries of its activities or its sympathizers.

Public Funding

Public funding barely covers one quarter of the associations questioned that were created after 14 January 2011. In most cases, it takes an in-kind form, not cash. For example, places provided to be used as headquarters for the association or its branches, enabling the association to benefit from public procedures for youth employment or providing some means of transport on the occasion of some activities. Some public institutions may cover some of the expenses, like food and water during activities (meals or coffee breaks). There is a division among association officials between those who refuse public funding and consider it a factor that limits the independence and neutrality of the association, those who accept it on certain terms, and also those who accept it without reservation and demand it as one of their rights.

Donations from Individuals

About two thirds of associations (sixty-five percent) are partially funded by virtue of donations from individuals. For certain categories of associations, especially scientific associations or associations of public nature, the donations come from members of the administrative board or personnel. They are mainly aimed at contributing to covering some of the vital expenses (like leasing fees). The donations received by charity associations usually come from individuals; apart from the mangers of the associations, who get receipts for their donations, they sometimes remain anonymous. Many of these associations receive transfers to their bank or postal accounts from people they do not know. Some charity associations received large sums of money from individuals paying their zakat.[14]

Moral Donations from People

Private and national moral donations from people do not represent a source of funding for most associations. Only one fifth of associations mention this as a funding source. Most of them, especially charity associations, state that funding is primarily in-kind and not in cash (food, stationery, and construction material).

Foreign Funding

Foreign funding is considered a qualitatively important source of funding. It is dominated by funding within partnership contracts with foreign juristic bodies, including international organizations like the United Nations, which intensified its interventions especially through the United Nations Development Program and the United Nations High Commissioner for Human Rights; regional organizations like the European Union; and various associations and organizations of different origins (American, German, Swiss, and Qatari). The percentage of associations that receive funding through partnership contracts with foreign juristic bodies has reached thirty percent, whereas ten percent

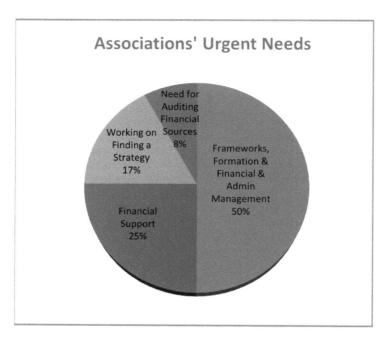

Associations' Urgent Needs

- Need for Auditing Financial Sources 8%
- Working on Finding a Strategy 17%
- Frameworks, Formation & Financial & Admin Management 50%
- Financial Support 25%

receive donations from foreign organizations
(affiliated with a certain country, or regional or international) which they use for spending acts (leasing places and paying wages) and acquiring equipment necessary for their activities. Some donations are in-kind, especially in the form of computers and other office supplies.

Less than one quarter of the sample of associations formed after 14 January 2011 state that their income comes from activities (for example, ticketed cultural and artistic events, selling products with a price that is higher than commercial prices in charity sales). The volume of these sales is not significant; it may not even cover the expenses of the event organized. Other resources may be added that come from various sources (eleven percent) including notarization contracts signed with different institutions, for example, communication institutions.

DISPOSITION OF MONEY IN ASSOCIATIONS: ISSUE OF SECURING TRANSPARENCY IN DISPOSITION OF ASSOCIATION MONEY

Fifty-seven percent of associations stressed the respect for procedures that decree number 88 in 2011, imposes on this issue; however, we find that only three percent of them actually declare financial data in the press or on their website.[15] Thirty-eight percent of associations state that they deposit their money in a bank account and that all the money is deposited in this account. Payments are made through checks that are signed by the head of the association and the treasurer. About nineteen percent of associations employ an accountant, and some associations (six percent) have income and expenditure that means they must employ the services of an auditor. Some reservations are subject to auditing approved by the association structure (five percent) or demanded by foreign financiers (less than two percent).

About eleven percent of associations declared that there are no measures to ensure transparency in spending association funds because there is no income.

ASSOCIATION NEEDS

NEEDS IN THE FIELD OF TRAINING AND CAPACITY BUILDING

Eighty-five percent of the associations in question stated that they have needs in the field of training and capacity building. At the forefront of these needs comes the need related to capacity building in the administrative and financial disposition of the association (fifty-five percent). This is because most association managers confess to a scarcity of knowledge among members of the administrative commission, in varying degrees, about aspects of administrative and financial disposition of the association. Improving their capacity in this regard is bound to reflect positively on the association's performance. On a second level, forty-six percent of associations questioned expressed their commission's and active personnel's need for structural training sessions in human rights, in order to strengthen their abilities in this regard; the same applies for environment associations in the field of preserving the environment. On a third level, thirty-two percent of the associations in question stated their need for receiving training on strategic planning. This indicates a shift in the mentality in newly formed associations, which seek to ensure their sustainability. Concerning the immense difficulties that some associations faced when seeking to prepare profiles in response to requests for offers suggested by foreign financiers, one quarter of associations questioned (twenty-five percent) expressed their need for capacity building in the field of preparing these profiles. This forced some of them to hire professionals to prepare profiles that would get accepted and overcome the ramified formalities and terms. More than fourteen percent of associations, especially those that include structural work within their basic work, asserted their need for training trainers in order to enable them to conduct structural training sessions organized by them at a reasonable financial cost.

The chart below illustrates the urgent need of associations for frameworks, formation, and financial and administrative management, which amounts to fifty percent of the total needs; this is a very important percentage, and it is an immediate and urgent issue. Financial support comes in second place with twenty-five percent, working on finding a strategy is next with seventeen percent, and the need for legal auditing of financial sources comes fourth place with eight percent.

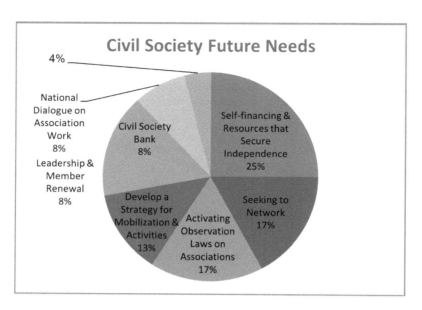

Civil Society Future Needs

- 4%
- National Dialogue on Association Work 8%
- Leadership & Member Renewal 8%
- Civil Society Bank 8%
- Self-financing & Resources that Secure Independence 25%
- Develop a Strategy for Mobilization & Activities 13%
- Activating Observation Laws on Associations 17%
- Seeking to Network 17%

NEEDS IN THE FIELD OF EXCHANGING INFORMATION, KNOWLEDGE, AND EXPERIENCES

Eighty-five percent of associations questioned stated that they have needs in the field of exchanging information, knowledge, and experiences. To be more specific, about fifty-five percent of the associations expressed their need for exchanging expertise and information with national associations with a similar specialization. Fifty-one percent of associations highlighted their eagerness to exchange expertise and information with foreign associations in the same field. Many indicators show the associations' desire to acquire information or to reach accurate information. Thirteen percent of associations expressed their need to access information banks affiliated with foreign associations and specialized international organizations that are related to their field of activity, while ten percent of associations emphasized their need to create a data bank.

NEEDS IN NETWORKING

One quarter of the associations questioned stated that they are not interested in networking (twenty-three percent), and eight percent of these associations emphasized their need to inventory specialized associations that they can network with, while thirty-eight percent clearly expressed their need for networking with all specialized associations in the association's field of activity. Some associations stipulated that the matter should be concerned with effective networking with specialized associations in the same field of activity as the association and not just a formality (twenty-three percent). As for the basic motives behind networking, they are respectively: exchanging logistical support with associations specialized in the same activity and located in other provinces (fourteen percent), strengthening its pressure force (eight percent), supporting the presence of the field of specialization on the national arena, for example defending issues concerning the environment (five percent of associations questioned).

The chart shows the future needs for the associations in question according to their standards. They are spearheaded by the need for self-financing and resources that secure independence (twenty-five percent), seeking to network and activating the observation laws on associations (seventeen percent), placing a strategy for mobilizing and activities (thirteen percent), in addition to needs that are not so urgent like renewal of leadership and members (eight percent), establishing a bank for civil society (eight percent), and launching a national dialogue surrounding association work (eight percent).

OTHER MISCELLANEOUS NEEDS

On the top of these needs are the ones related to funding. We notice in this regard that some associations crave funding regardless of its origin. If we wanted to be precise, we would note that most associations seek to obtain public funding (fifty-five percent), while forty-three percent of them seek to gather grants and donations from national citizens, and forty-one percent of associations hope to obtain project funding within a partnership framework with foreign juristic bodies. In addition to financial needs, an urgent need for thirty-eight percent of associations is acquiring an adequate headquarters for the association's activities. In the same context, twenty-six percent of associations stress the need to obtain equipment that would enhance the association's activities, while more than thirteen percent stress the need to hire salaried workers to ensure the continuity and sustainability of the association's activities. Less urgent needs are added to all of this, like reinforcing the association with scientific expertise (seven percent), and the need to access information whose availability is a vital element for the association's work (six percent).

GENERAL SURROUNDINGS FOR ASSOCIATIONS

Associations work in a general framework that they cannot be separated from. This framework represents, to a large extent, one of the association's strength indicators. In addition to its internal capacity, measuring the importance of an association, or lack thereof, depends on its external capacity to be affected by the context in which it is present and to affect it. This reality can be represented through a simple graph, made up of a circle with three arrows. Inside the circle is the concerned association, the up arrow indicates authority (and administration), while the down arrow indicates citizens (and targets of the association's work), as for the horizontal arrow, it represents the association's relationship with its associational, national and international surroundings.

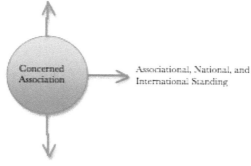

Authority (and Administration)

Concerned Association

Associational, National, and International Standing

Citizens and Targets

RELATIONSHIP WITH CITIZENS

The relationship between citizens and associations seems problematic.

From the citizen's standpoint, we notice:

- Citizens' wariness, especially on the basis level, of associations. This goes back to the legacy of the former regime, to which we can also attribute the following remarks:
- The bad image of women's rights organizations in the minds of many citizens.
- Lack of knowledge about successful association experiences in Tunisia before the revolution and the weakness of the media in current experiences (weakness in appraisal).
- Citizens notice the weakness of the effect of projects and association work on the realistic and concrete level (there are some associations where you cannot separate their work from political work such as human rights associations).
- Not separating, in the minds of many, association work from political work. This is enforced by the associations' great intervention in political work.

From the associations' standpoint, we emphasize:

- Weakness of social rooting and proximity to citizens, especially those who belong to disadvantaged social classes. This is enforced by an elitist rhetoric adopted by some associations.

- Associations' inability to influence through their projects and work on the realistic level, which seems to be clearly observed by citizens.
- Concentration of most of the associations' work in certain geographical areas.

RELATIONSHIP WITH AUTHORITIES

Two main characteristics distinguish the scene in Tunisia after 14 January in regard to associations' relationship with authorities:

The First Characteristic is Independence from Political Authorities

This trait characterizes the association scene in Tunisia after 14 January in its entirety without any specification. Although not entirely wrong, considering that it expresses the reality of many associations formed after 14 January and a few of those formed under the former regime, it remains relative to a large extent. Although most associations in Tunisia were mere democracy displays and mounts for certain influential people in the former regime, matters have turned around today. Alongside associations that were independent of the regime and formed during its reign–there were a few–a majority of associations have emerged that are distinguished by their independent work and cautious to preserve this trait to an extent that this sometimes becomes an obstacle for them to carry out their work and communicate with various entities, for example, the administration or partners, as will be shown later. This trait must be put into perspective by two major considerations. A large number of associations are nothing but authoritarian tools in the hands of political parties, especially a large number of charity associations and "leagues for protecting the revolution." On the other hand, this may be due to the nature of the phase the country is experiencing where associations find themselves forced to take one side or the other of the political and ideological division that the country is going through.

The Second Characteristic is the Existence of a Clear Political Recognition in Associations' Role and Importance

The fact that there is a clear recognition for the role of associations after 14 January is rarely ever disputed. However, this recognition remains insufficient, considering that the relationship between the administration and associations is characterized by mutual caution. This caution is a result of the remnants of the former era that lacked a participatory tradition and where the relationship between the two sides was characterized by confrontation. Therefore, associations remain cautious of intervention in their independence and refuse to cooperate with the authorities or seek their help, forgetting that independence does not mean refusing all help from the government, but rather the refusal of help on the condition of supporting all government position and acts.[16] As for the administration, they criticize associations for their abundance and dispersion on the one hand, and their insufficient expertise, professionalism, and effectiveness on the other hand, in addition to the evident political bias of some of them. All of these are reasons stand as obstacles for the administration to effectively cooperate with associations.

Although this confrontational atmosphere has not prevented the accomplishment of important cooperation experiences between associations and the authority such as the experience of the National Constituent Assembly that put forward procedures to interact with associations regarding the preparation of draft laws, we notice the weakness of the administration's incorporation of civil society in preparing government projects and plans. There is also a lack of reliance on the accomplishments of associations through their studies and suggestions, in addition to the administration's refusal, in many cases, to enable associations to access vital information for their work, as some association managers asserted. One study[17] finds that twelve percent of associations questioned asserted their participation in regional or local administrational decision-making through attending consultations and formal meetings, and that six out of 128 associations played the role of mediator during local or regional conflicts. On the national level, some associations stated they exercised pressure on the National Constituent Assembly to emphasize some articles in the constitution. Some also played the role of monitoring and applying media pressure on some legislative acts in the National Constituent Assembly, such as preparing the law concerning the Independent High Commission for Elections.

Indeed, if this characterization applies to the general relationship between the authorities and civil society, then the weakness of communication, whose manifestation we have addressed, remains more tangible on the regional and local level due to the absence of government institutions on these levels at the current time. It is also due to doubts that the existing structures' represent the government and not of one of the political parties.

This situation seems hard to circumvent, especially with the existing legal mechanisms that regulate interaction between civil society and the administration. Therefore, excluding some strong associations like the Tunisian League for Human Rights, Commission of Lawyers, and the General Union for Tunisian Workers, which have become an essential component of political society (parties sponsoring national dialogue), the effect of associations on decision-making and political orientation remains intangible enough, especially when many associations overlook affecting decision-makers in their objectives.

Decisions to Stop 157 Associations from Carrying Out Activities

The crisis cell, charged with examining the security situation in the country (especially after the increase in terrorist operations), recommended on 20 July 2014 stopping the activities of associations that were proven to be involved in funding and aiding terrorism, or that were suspected of such. The government endorsed this recommendation and asked each governor, in his jurisdiction, to enforce the decision to stop these associations and, according to the authority of each governor, to take necessary measures to maintain public order. These conservative procedures aimed to verify, especially by confiscating the funding sources of these associations, their potential relations with some terrorist parties or elements, and monitor their activities on the conceptual level and the public projects level.

This procedure, which included associations that have religious and charitable dimensions like "Our Mosques Association," "Islamic Guidance Association," "Islamic Boy Scout Association," and "Legacy of Prophecy Association" is bound to assert the relationship of some new associations with political parties and violence. However, stopping these associations from carrying out their activities according to suspicions based on their designations may pose a threat to rights and freedoms, especially as the decree for associations stipulated that associations cannot be stopped without a judicial order.

RELATIONSHIP WITH THE NATIONAL AND INTERNATIONAL ASSOCIATIONAL SPHERE

The associational sphere in Tunisia after 14 January is distinguished by two main traits in this regard:

- First: the vast experience of many old associations that new associations may benefit from, especially in networking.
- Second: the large offer of technical and financial partnership from foreign institutions and associations.

However, several obstacles prevent associations from benefiting from these two factors.

Three facts prevent associations from benefiting from the first factor:

1. Division of civil society into two major poles: "the modern pole" on the one hand and the "traditional pole" on the other, and the fueling of the conflict between these two poles on the fieldwork level. This associational division, which reflects a division in society and politics, hinders the possibility of some associations agreeing on common goals and joint projects.
2. Lack of complete knowledge about important national and international association experiences among many members and managers of new associations.
3. Despite the launch of the networking phenomenon in Tunisia after the revolution, it remains limited in its reach[18] and restricted to partial works and projects, where they exist. This is not a complete use of the

stipulations of the decree of 2011 which enabled associations to operate as formal networks.

Partnership offers and aid provision also suffer problems, the most important of which may be:

From the standpoint of associations:

1. Exaggerated caution from some associations, especially new ones, of foreign partnership which may be due, in part, to the legacy of the former regime.
2. Difficulty in communicating with technical and financial partners. Perhaps what best explains this, in addition to the first point, is the weakness of the internal governance of associations and lack of communication skills among their members.

From the standpoint of those who present partnership offers:

1. Usually, they present offers that do not go beyond partial partnership surrounding certain projects and with a complete absence of interest in developing the association's self-capabilities on a permanent basis.
2. Parties that intervene on an international level continue to give priority to associations situated in large and coastal cities, and their interest in inland areas remains limited.
3. Profiles for offers suggested by foreign financiers are complex, which means associations need to build capacity in the field of preparing profiles. [19]

ENDNOTES

[1] It resumed its activities after 14 January 2014.

[2] If we add to it the three provinces that constitute Greater Tunis (Arian, Ben Arous, and Manouba), the total number of associations of Greater Tunis would be over 4,975 associations up to July 2014.

[3] Arab Institute for Human Rights, field study surrounding Tunisian associations formed after 14 January 2011 and that are concerned in economic and social development, human rights, and transparency in Nabeul, Sfax, Kef, and Medenine provinces ; prepared by a team under the supervision of Dr. Fadel Balibish, September 2013 pp 18-19.

[4] Ibid, p20.

[5] *Al-Raed Al-Rasmi*, 63, (22 December 1959).

[6] *Al-Raed Al-Rasmi*, 74, (30 September 2011).

[7] European Union, Formulation mission, Support program for Tunisian civil society, *Diagnostic report on Tunisian civil society*, March 2012, p8.

[8] European Union, March 2012, p8

[9] www.ifeda.org.tn

[10] Euro-Mediterranean Human Rights Network, *Establishment of a directory of associations and NGOs in Tunisia to strengthen the capacity of NGOs to influence and take action to defend Human Rights,* October 2011.

[11] Hatem M'rad, "La société civile tunisienne : spontanéité, indépendance et résistance", *Le Courrier del'Atlas,* Tuesday 2nd April 2013, http://www.lecourrierdel'atlas.com/448202042013Tunisie-La-Societe-civile-tunisienne-spontanéité-independance-et-resistance.html

[12] -http:eeas.europa.eu/delegation/tunisia/project/overview/civilsocietyfr.htn.
-Aide mémoire "Support for Tunisian civil society -Dialogue and coordination", European Union delegation in Tunisia, November 2011.
-Diagnostic report on Tunisian civil society, European Union delegation in Tunisia, March 2012.

[13] A few associations revealed their annual financial reports, donation receipts, or membership fees.

[14] One of the managers at the Compassionate Hearts Association in Sfax, stated that his association received a sum of money that exceeded four thousand dinars from an individual wanting to pay his zakat.

[15] One of the mangers at a well-known association told us in a recorded statement that his association's declaration of some of its financial data in the press or on the association's website was met with disapproval and criticism from some of the managers of other associations who did not like, as he put it, establishing a tradition of revealing the true financial status of associations.

[16] European Union, March 2012, p18

[17] Study by Arab Institute for Human Rights, p27.

[18] A study by the Arab Institute for Human Rights shows that twenty-three percent of associations questioned do not desire networking, and thirty-eight percent expressed their need for networking which implies their incapability of realizing it.

[19] Study by the Arab Institute for Human Rights, p38.

Changing Realities for Non-Governmental Organizations in Yemen post-2011

Majid Almzhadji

SUMMARY

This report provides an extensive overview of non-governmental organizations in Yemen. Focusing on the period between 2011 and 2014, it includes descriptions, statistics, and an extended account of these organizations' current reality. This report aims to analyze multiple sources of data and information in an attempt to understand the work environment of these organizations, their complexities, their relationships with each other and various institutions, as well as the agendas that inform their work, goals, and activities. It examines the political and ideological effects of political parties on organizations and activists, their relationship and engagement with these effects, and the controversial relationship between the state and these organizations. Moreover, this report also aims to shed light on the funding process, the most important international donors, as well as the nature of regional and international relations through which Yemeni NGOs may become involved with counterpart organizations abroad or with other countries.

INTRODUCTION

The unification of North Yemen and South Yemen into one state in 1990 represented the end of an era of totalitarianism and the start of a new rule that espoused a liberal, democratic identity. For the first time, Yemenis had the right to organize in a variety of ways, the most important being though NGOs. Yet, though they had the right to form NGOs—one of the most important forms of organization, and one citizens across the world use to defend their interests—civil society did not develop deep roots in Yemen. Instead, political parties continued to polarize, and people remained bound to traditional tribal and clan forms of social organization. These were more appealing means for people to use to advocate for their interests, more appealing than NGOs, which were surrounded by suspicion, seen by the public as mere tools of the foreign countries that fund them, and subject to veiled hostility from authorities, which isolated them further and made them a less viable option for organizing.

Yet this did not prevent NGOs from becoming a significant feature of public life in Yemen, nor did it prevent them from improving their activities, especially between the late 1990s and 2011. As a result of the Arab Spring, which affected many countries in the region, Yemen went through significant transformations that impacted all aspects of life.

The decade prior to 2011 was a golden period for NGOs in Yemen, in which their public role improved in multiple areas of their purview. Though these institutions faced accusations of spying, suspicions of corruption, and poor institutional regulation, they established themselves as a prime platform through which many parts of Yemeni society expressed themselves. They also posed a real concern for state authority, which was becoming progressively more authoritarian. While the state presented itself as a democratic one, in truth it relied on control, regarded any independent body not under its control with suspicion, and consistently dealt with matters through security measures.

The situation in Yemen changed completely after 2011. Ruling political alliances cracked and reformed, a new form of governance began after former President Ali Abdullah Saleh was ousted, and Yemen entered a transitional phase that continues today. Everything is up for reconsideration during this period, from the constitution, to the form of the state, and relationships between various civil entities.

These rapid transformations threw non-governmental organizations into confusion after 2011. They seemed unable to change their reading of the events that had happened and continued to unfold, or to present new agendas that could respond to the new changes and challenges that had arisen.

This confusion was due to several factors, a significant one being the deep crisis in the country; the failure of the transitional period has clearly affected the environment that NGOs work within. As regional and sectarian identities emerged as a crucial factor in social and political relations, nationalist ties among Yemenis have weakened, and people are less able to rely on tools of public service, such as civil society work and NGOs. The increasing shift from the national identity to pre-national identities in order to protect private interests has caused people to turn away from visions of civil society based on equal citizenship. In an environment of increasing violence, widespread political corruption, and polarized identities, NGOs have grown weaker and their public role has diminished. This has been accompanied by structural weakness, and the corruption of activists, as political parties involve them in the transitional period —either by appointing them in high government positions, or by giving them lucrative political roles, as in the National Conference—which has ultimately hindered NGOs' involvement and overall performance since 2011.

LEGAL CONTEXT

After South Yemen and North Yemen unified in 1990, the Republic of Yemen went through a democratic transformation. A constitution was created for the newly unified country, to guarantee parties, political associations, trade unions, professional, scientific, cultural and social associations the freedom to form, and to guarantee various freedoms and human rights, and protect them from being violated.

Subsequent amendments to the constitution of 1990 did not impinge upon these basic rights. Article 58 of the constitution guarantees the right to establish non-governmental organizations in Yemen, and states, "In as much as it is not contrary to the constitution, citizens may organize themselves along political, professional and union lines. They have the right to form associations in scientific, cultural, social and national unions in a way that serves the goals of the constitution. The state shall guarantee these rights, and shall take the necessary measures to enable citizens to exercise them. The state shall guarantee freedom for the political, trade, cultural, scientific and social organizations."[1]

Despite guarantees provided by the constitution, NGOs in Yemen are subject to a wide range of laws regulating their activities by field, and this amount of legislation interferes with their activities. The degree of legislation related to aspects of the organization's activity delineates zones of freedom "according to the organization's area of activity, whether 'union related, agricultural, charitable, political, human rights, trade... etc,'"[2] as opposed to upholding their freedom in principle. Law No. 1 of 2001 on Civil Associations and Institutions, as well as the Prime Minister's Decree No. 129 of 2004 on implementing regulations for that law, are considered the most important laws related to civil society activity in Yemen. Other important laws related to regulating those organizations' activities include:

1. The Constitution of the Republic of Yemen.
2. Law No. 39 on Cooperative Unions and Associations.
3. Law No. 35 of 2002 on the Regulation of Labor Unions.
4. Law No. 38 on the Chambers of Commerce, Industry, and their Public Union.

Activists are subject to laws regulating civil society as well as to provisions of the Penal Code. This is a legal inconsistency, which restricts freedoms and limits the activities of civil society actors.[3]

According to the Law of Civil Associations, obtaining a license for an NGO requires the following:

1. A request to establish an association or a union, signed by the founding members or their representatives; the founding members must complete legal procedures and hold a meeting to establish the civil or cooperative association.
2. Required documents: articles of incorporation, request to establish the organization or the union, draft statute, draft of the draft statute, list of the founders' names and signatures.
3. Procedures: study the request submitted by the founder; review the draft of the draft statute; make amendments according to the provisions of the law if possible; verify the organization's headquarters; release an announcement calling to hold an annual founding meeting; supervise

the meeting; announce results of the meeting; grant the license/license renewal.[4]

STATISTICS ON NGOS IN YEMEN

There are currently more than nine thousand NGOs in Yemen registered with the Ministry of Social Affairs and Labor. There were 8,317 registered NGOs at the end of 2011, and 9,700 as of 31 December 2013, which means that the number of registered NGOs increased by 1,383 between 2011 and 2013, according to general statistics on NGOs issued by the Information Department. The Information Department falls within the Social Development Sector at the Ministry of Social Affairs, a government agency concerned with issuing licenses in accordance with Law No. 1 of 2001 on Civil Institutions and Associations.

The Ministry for Non-Governmental Organizations' official classification system covers a wide range of organizations, including trade unions, cooperative unions, civil institutions and associations. As per recent official statistics issued by the ministry, NGOs are classified into two groups. The first includes cooperative unions and associations, which are in turn divided into general, agricultural, consumer, residential, fishing, and craft associations. The second includes civil institutions and associations, which are divided into charities, institutions, social, cultural, professional, and scientific associations, fraternities, friendships, clubs, and forums.

However, the classification criteria are vague; for example, the difference between a civil association (classified as professional) and a cooperative association (classified as a craft) is unclear.

In Yemen, public perception is that "non-governmental organizations" are those that generally deal with human rights, trade union, and development. This is related to how the public understands these organizations' public role, especially given the number of human rights organizations defending freedom of expression. The Journalists Syndicate was at the vanguard of such organizations, particularly prior to 2011, when it was the first line of defense against violations committed by former President Ali Abdullah Saleh's regime.

Overall, the number of officially registered organizations has increased. According to official statistics, there were 9,210 registered organizations at the end of 2012, of which 1,899 were classified as cooperative unions and associations, 6,893 as civil associations and institutions and their unions, and 418 as branches of civil associations and institutions in the provinces outside the capital.

By 31 December 2013, a year later, there were 490 additional organizations registered: twenty-six new cooperative unions and associations, 463 new civil associations and institutions and their unions, and one new branch in the provinces, bringing the total number of NGOs to 9,700 by the end of 2013.[5]

Among the twenty-six cooperative associations registered in 2013, there were seventeen new agricultural associations registered in 2013, followed by nine residential associations, and no new associations registered in any of the four other categories. Among the 463 civil associations and institutions registered in 2013, there were 193 new social associations, followed by 125 institutions, and 115 charitable organizations, fifteen forums, five scientific associations, five cultural associations, three professional associations, one friendship association, and one general union. There was also only one new branch of an association registered, one affiliated with a social association in the Ma'rib province.

Social associations, institutions, and charities form the greatest percentage of new organizations; social associations and charities fall under a framework of takaful solidarity, and usually have a large presence. These associations have social roles, are made up of people in rural areas or residential neighborhoods, and advocate for people's rights to access and obtain services. Human rights and development organizations form the second largest group of organizations registered in 2013, while organizations with special interests are rare. Most organizations tend to have vague aims, which enables them to work in multiple fields. This is mainly due to the fact that "activists, 'the founders,' of these organizations, lack specialization and professionalism, especially when it comes to setting goals that include social, charitable, human rights, and other aims. This is exacerbated by weak efforts to facilitate networking, as well as a lack of specialization, which would help meet social needs."[6]

There is clearly an inadequate geographic distribution of NGOs, and they do not serve all parts of the community equally. NGOs are concentrated in the capital and provincial centers, "as they work in similar sectors and on similar programs. Some sectors of society are still far from these organizations' activities, and others are just beginning to be served by them."[7]

NGOs' ADMINISTRATIVE AND INSTITUTIONAL FRAMEWORK

The Law on Civil Associations and Institutions imposes institutional and administrative policies on organizations in Yemen, regulating their operations. The founders are considered "owners" of the institution or the association, as they signed the articles of incorporation; they owned the funds paid to establish the organization, and thus have complete authority over its activities. The most common institutional framework of organizations, which must be approved by the ministry, also requires the existence of a Board of Trustees (BOT), which consists of seven or eleven members, and must include the founders. The BOT has managerial authority over the organization's activities, including appointing an Executive Director, and policy-making for the organization.[8]

Under the statute, the BOT's role is only symbolic; trustees must be appointed by the founders, and must apply for the license by law. The founders have full administrative powers, and in most organizations the BOT does not play an active role.

The founder or founders manage the organization entirely, and are not actually accountable to, or assessed by, the Board of Trustees or any other body. NGOs usually have a director, CEO, and a staff member to perform secretarial tasks. The number of other employees is dependent on their ability to obtain funding from donors for specific programs; they would appoint a finance officer, a media officer, and other employees as the program requires. In most cases, the founders appoint a finance officer and media officer to serve more than one program within the organization. Organizations often hire contract employees to implement specific funded projects. They stay with the organization as long as funding is available and until the project is completed; however, they are not permanent staff.

For example, the Arab Al-Shaqaik Forum for Human Rights, which carried out a three-year program combatting violence against women, used to have at least nine employees, as well as about six contracted lawyers in the provinces. Employees included the director, a finance officer, project coordinator, media and advocacy officer, psychologist, archivist, lawyer (as head of the legal team), logistics officer, and a driver. At the end of the project, which lasted for three years, the number of employees was decreased to two: the president and a secretary.[9]

There are several reasons for the decrease in number of staff. The end of the project on violence against women, which was financed by the Dutch government, coincided with the events of 2011. Staff members were preoccupied with the escalating events, and did not submit funding applications for new projects, which would have enabled the forum to maintain a relatively high number of employees. Furthermore, the forum's financial manager, Anis Al-Asidi, was killed while participating in demonstrations against former President Ali Abdullah Saleh. This was a blow to the organization, its employees, and the general work environment. One volunteer stayed with the forum for a year after this, until she married and left the organization.

The Yemeni Observatory for Human Rights and the National Organization for Defending Rights and Freedoms (HOOD) are two other organizations whose administrative structures have changed depending on the projects they undertake, though both organizations consistently employ a director and a CEO. The Yemeni Observatory currently employs five employees including the CEO, while the director remotely supervises the organization's work. HOOD has a staff of seven, including the director and the CEO. The recently founded Muwatana Organization for Human Rights only employs director and a CEO, who are the founders of the organization, and has no other employees due to lack of financial resources.

Other organizations, such as the Democratic School, operate without a CEO, particularly when the director plays an active role in the organization.

This general administrative structure is typical for NGOs in Yemen, and remained virtually unchanged after 2011; there is still a need for administrative staff, and the number of employees in a given organization is still based on their funding and programs.

Yet these organizations frequently suffer from mismanagement. They tend to lack institutional frameworks, transparency, adequate education and experience, and teamwork training, and are detached from society and other organizations. They also suffer from external difficulties, primarily the distrust of the state and citizens. The hostile propaganda waged against these organizations by traditional conservative powers has sown distrust and caused them to be surrounded with suspicion, especially with regards to their foreign funders and management of resources. As a result, these associations and institutions have been unable to obtain community support and contributions from the private sector in Yemen to finance their activities, and have failed to communicate with the public and each other.

NGOs POST-2011: FOUNDERS, ROLES, INTERESTS, RELATIONSHIPS AND ADMINISTRATIVE AND INSTITUTIONAL STRUCTURES

The grip of security and politics—which had long determined organizations' ability to obtain a legal license and establish themselves,[10] especially political and human rights organizations—was significantly eased after the 2011 revolution. This coincided with the rise of Yemeni Islamists, namely the Yemeni Congregation for Reform (Al-Islah), who gained power in the political vacuum. It was an ideal opportunity for activists and interested parties to obtain licenses for new organizations, as this process had been tightly restrained prior to 2011.

The process of giving permits to new NGOs became significantly less complicated after 2011, as complications had been closely linked to the regime's security decisions. The permit-granting process improved significantly after the transitional period, when all parties signed the Gulf Cooperation Council (GCC) initiative and the national unity government was formed.

Many individuals who hope to establish new organizations are activists affiliated with the political Islamic movement. This cannot be confirmed statistically, but estimated by examining the backgrounds of activists who recently began to work in civil society. Many are not activists or members of the Al-Islah Party, as can best be determined from their political positions, but part of a broader movement supporting the Islamists.

Islamists were not the only ones interested in applying for licenses. Other political movements, such as those affiliated with the General People's Congress (GPC), headed by the former president, and all other parties, were also interested. Independent political activists who could not obtain a license for their organization under Saleh, such as Abdulrashid Al-Faqih and Radhiyah Al-Mutawakkil who co-founded the Muwatana Organization for Human Rights, were also interested. After setbacks under Saleh, they did everything they could to obtain a license for an institution that had previously operated without one.

It was clear that these organizations' activities could play an important role in politics. Discovering the role they had prior to 2011 was the prime factor in people's sudden "politicized" enthusiasm for founding new organizations, along with a desire to "obtain funding" and use funds provided by international donors. There is a common perception in Yemen that NGO work is a quick route to wealth, particularly given weak monitoring tools and lack of transparency for their work.[11]

As a result of the increasing political polarization that affected NGOs, the role and value of civil society work declined significantly after 2011. Many organizations became political platforms for various parties, while most youth movements—which had been founded during the popular uprising in Yemen in 2011—did not end up becoming NGOs, or even unstructured youth initiatives, though they did maintain a public role. One prominent youth initiative among those in Change Square in Sanaa is an exception to this; its role in the media has increased under the hashtag "#SUPPORTYEMEN." This group organized its first activity, a film about the revolution, in September 2011. Building on this, it uploaded a collection of videos on YouTube, which soon became popular. The initiative focuses on the civil society aspect of the revolution through these videos. Three years later, the initiative became an NGO, officially registering with the Ministry of Social Affairs and Labor in July 2014. Although, legally, Support Yemen is a civil institution, as dictated by law, its founders describe it as "media collective" that shares issues of concern with the media. Support Yemen's website describes the group as "a media campaign that supports peaceful struggle of the Yemeni people to achieve freedom, equality and social justice,"[12] emphasizing that it does not work on these issues nor speak on behalf of those who struggle with them; instead, it helps people speak up for themselves.

Male and female activists of Support Yemen emphasize their identity as young people, and that they are a civil movement intimately bound to their history of struggle, which began with the 2011 revolution. They describe themselves as follows: "We are young Yemeni female and male organizers, activists, journalists, videographers, photographers, web designers, and bloggers. We were, and still are, inseparable from the peaceful popular struggle on the street in Yemen since 3 February 2011. Now, after all this time since the first demonstration calling for change emerged, the peaceful struggle movement is in dire need of effective means to deliver objective, transparent, and clear messages to countries in the region and the international community about the nature of the peaceful popular struggle in Yemen, in terms of freedom and change. It needs to convey what this movement—and the entire population of Yemen—has been facing since February 2011. This is where the idea of "Support Yemen—Break the Barrier of Silence" came from: to communicate messages supporting the struggle to build a civil state, in which the constitution guarantees freedom, equality, and social justice for the Yemeni people, in a way that preserves Yemeni society's sectarian, partisan, and religious diversity and pluralism, consistent with the state of equality, democracy, and rule of law.[13]

Support Yemen was formed and developed by young people who came together during the popular uprising, yet now it is a civil society initiative. Even though it must be registered as a civil society organization in order to obtain legal status, it does not want to be regarded as such. According to Sarah Gamal, one of Support Yemen's ten founders, "We do not see ourselves as a civil society group, but as media collective. We do not receive funds from any entity, instead we provide services and get funds that way."[14]

The essence of Support Yemen's work is related to the experience of its activists, most of whom are filmmakers. As a media collective, it produces participatory films where the people themselves, not the activists, are the hero. Their goal is amplify unheard voices in society and on issues. Training—that is, turning young activists into a cadre of filmmakers—is another issue Support Yemen is concerned with.

Support Yemen's institutional structure differs from other civil society organizations as well. It consists of a board of directors, which includes the ten founders: four young women and six young men. There is also an executive director, a media team, a team for production and research, and finally the membership base. The positions of executive director, media team manager, and director of production and research are all appointed in an annual election.

Support Yemen refuses to accept external funding, and so it must provide its equipment and ensure its activities continue through donated tools and volunteers; only the producers receive salaries. Support Yemen describes its policy as a "policy of collecting resources, based on sustainability, creativity, participation, and independence."[15]

Support Yemen is a youth initiative that challenges the prevailing definition of NGOs in Yemen. It aims to establish its own version of public presence and internal dynamics, even if it must conform with the official legal definition of a civil institution under Yemeni legislation. The organization's founders believe that through their relationship with the public and various issues, they can offer a different take on civil society work. They believe they can be truly independent, free from the burden of funding agendas that have corrupted civil society work in Yemen in the past.

NGOs' GOALS, INTERESTS, AND ACTIVITIES: BEFORE AND AFTER 2011

Most human rights NGOs in Yemen—including the Yemeni Observatory for Human Rights,[16] the National Organization for Defending Rights and Freedoms (HOOD),[17] the Yemeni Center for Human Rights, the Yemeni Organization for Human Rights, and the Yemen Center for Human Rights Studies[18]—focus primarily on political and civil rights, nearly to the exclusion of economic and social rights. They work towards their goals by providing judicial assistance, advocacy, and working on amending legislation to be more sensitive to human rights. The Arab Sisters Forum[19] is concerned with political and civil rights, and focuses on women's rights in terms of political participation and discrimination-based violence. Two other organizations in the field of women's rights are the Arab Institution for Human Rights and the Women's Forum for Studies and Training,[20] which primarily focus on advocating for women's issues in the democratic process and civil society, by holding discussions and publishing reports and studies.[21]

These organizations engaged in more activities and services prior to 2011, when the country was more politically and socially stable, and the political system made defining NGO's roles and activities against violations clearer. As a result of political, social, and sectarian divisions that grew deeper after the 2011 revolution, activists and people in charge of organizations developed political and ideological affiliations. Many became involved with the path to democratic transition; general instability provided an opportunity to advance politically, which resulted in fierce competition. As different political powers were divided, organizations had less of a presence and engaged in fewer activities. Furthermore, the National Dialogue Conference,[22] which consisted of over 550 members, both men and women, and lasted for about a year, included leaders from most NGOs in Yemen. This delayed many of the NGOs' activities, except those related to training or the conference itself and its promotion.

Several organizations work in awareness-raising and training, including the Aswan Center for Social Research and Studies.[23] The Human Rights Information and Training Center (HRITC) is at the vanguard of the field; established in the mid 1990s, it is one of the oldest NGOs in Yemen. HRITC focuses on giving activists training in human rights information and skills in several fields. It has also issued reports on how objective civil and state media was during elections, especially prior to 2011. One of the most important activities of the HRITC—along with the Arab Sisters Forum—was issuing "shadow" reports. These were issued in parallel to government reports about the state of human rights, which were submitted to the United Nations Human Rights Council in Geneva. The reports covered issues such as how much of the implementation of the Convention on the Elimination of all Forms of

Discrimination Against Women (CEDAW), torture, and political and civil rights. A comprehensive report on human rights was also periodically released over several years, particularly before 2011. Yemen did not regularly submit parallel "shadow" reports after 2011, due to the transitional nature of the regime.

There are also more specialized NGOs, aimed at specific sectors. The Civil Direction Foundation (CDF)[24] works on election observation and training, as well as on social issues such as marginalization and women's issues. The Democracy School[25] is an old organization, and although it has fairly general aims, in practice it only works on children's issues. It established a "children's parliament," and is one of the top organizations in the field of children's rights, along with SEYAJ Organization for Childhood Protection.[26]

Other organizations, such as the Association for Rehabilitation and Care for the Disabled and the Yemeni Association for the Care and Rehabilitation of the Blind, provide services for groups with special needs. Some organizations, such as the Yemen Family Care Association (YFCA), work only on family, motherhood and reproductive health issues; the YFCA is considered one of the top organizations in the country in the field of family health services.[27] Other organizations, such as the Association for Women and Children's Development (SOUL), focus on women's development and training.

While NGOs in Yemen are engaged with a broad range of concerns and activities, the vast majority of activities focus on education, awareness or training. Although these activities are important, most focus on the organizations' own presence, which weakens both their outcomes and the public's opinion of them. Most awareness-raising activities support the common perception that NGOs are elite organizations, whose staff never leave their hotel rooms.

YEMENI NGOS: POOR COOPERATION AND COMPLICATED RELATIONS

Confronted with the security escalations in late 2006, a number of NGOs with a common interest in human rights established a coalition to take a unified stance and collective action against increasing violations. This came against the backdrop of the repression of the peaceful movement in Southern Yemen, human rights and humanitarian repercussions of wars in Saada between the government and the Houthis in Northern Yemen, and multiple violations against the press and human rights activists, which had reached a peak.

This new and voluntary form of organization was called the Coalition of Civilian Society Organization ("UMAM," for its Arabic acronym),[28] and was not connected to any funding programs. It sought to establish common positions and protests, including demonstrations and sit-ins protesting various issues for more than a year.

Yet due to political differences between parties over certain issues, the coalition did not last. As a result of competition between coalition members, and the desire of some parties in the coalition to use the its symbolic value in certain issues, this cooperation between Yemeni organizations broke down, and the coalition soon ceased all activities.[29] UMAM represents a brief, though intense, example of how cooperation between Yemeni NGOs could end, as these relationships are subject to complications and conflicts between personal and public interests.

The work environment for NGOs in Yemen is generally more competitive than cooperative. Yet this does not mean that joint work—implementing joint campaigns under joint programs, for example—falls under the same funding source. Relationships between organizations are ultimately determined by personal relationships, and the political background of the activists who founded them.

Personal relationships and individual political backgrounds seem to play a key role in whether relationships between organizations progress or falter, as seen in several Yemeni NGOs. The Yemeni Center for Civil Rights—a relatively new organization, established towards the end of last decade—has a close cooperative relationship with the Yemeni Observatory for Human Rights, and the Human Rights Information and Training Center. The founder of Yemeni Center for Civil Rights, Nour Al-Din Al-Azazi, has the same left-leaning political background as the founders of the other two organizations.

Other cooperative relationships between newer and more established organizations are based on stewardship. Some new NGOs are established under the support and care of larger and older organizations; sometimes, the founders of these organizations are former or current members of the older NGOs. For example, the Yemeni Group of Transparency and Impartiality is run by Tawfiq Albazigy, an activist from Human Rights Information and Training Center (HRITC). As the parent organization, and one of the largest NGOs in Yemen, HRITC provided important support for the new organization. In another example, the Prisoner Organization was founded by lawyer Abdulrahman Barman, who is still active in National Organization for Defending Rights and Freedoms (HOOD), which offers the new organization support and opportunities for cooperation.

INTERNATIONAL LAW AND HUMAN RIGHTS IN YEMENI NGOs MISSION STATEMENTS

The Universal Declaration of Human Rights features centrally in most Yemeni NGOs' mission statements. For example, the National Organization for Defending Rights and Freedoms (HOOD) writes,

HOOD is a nonprofit NGO, committed to defending and advocating for victims of abuses by providing them with legal assistance, and by uncovering violations and exposing those who commit them to the public. We are committed to spreading awareness of legal and human rights, to encourage respect for human rights and defend them.[30]

Human rights have an even clearer role in how the Human Rights Information and Training Center describes itself, as a private, non-profit NGO with complete political neutrality, which does not fall under any partisan or non-partisan entity. It is think tank aimed at promoting values of human rights in Yemen and the Arab world, and committed to all international agreements, conventions, and declarations of human rights issued by the United Nations.[31]

In contrast, the Yemen Family Care Association's mission statement does not explicitly reference the Universal Declaration of Human Rights, or Convention on the Elimination of all Forms of Discrimination Against Women (CEDAW), although the ideas within these declarations feature prominently.

The Yemeni Family Care Association is dedicated to improving the lives of women, children, and other community groups in Yemen, through programs that offer service and education and spread awareness. It is also committed to related capacity-building and advocacy programs, so that all segments of society can enjoy stability, health and well-being. The Yemeni Family Care Association (YFCA) believes in women's right to family planning and birth control, and their right to access legal means to avoid unwanted pregnancies. YFCA will continue to work hard, in order to provide relevant and reliable information to residents in the remote, rural, poor, and marginalized areas.[32]

The Democracy School, an organization dedicated to children's issues, does not explicitly reference human and children's rights in its mission statement: "The Democracy School is a non-profit NGO that seeks to create groups that engage in democratic and civil society work through various activities, to train people for future leadership." It presents itself as "a non-profit NGO that educates people and raises awareness about human rights, democratic rights, and 'the right of the child' in accordance with decree No. 199 of 2002 from the Minister of Social Affairs."[33]

Human rights and humanitarian international law are driving factors for many NGOs in Yemen. Regardless of their specific field or scope of interest, many NGOs were established to bridge the gap between the principles of human rights and actual law and reality in Yemen.

NGOs' ACTIVITIES AND PUBLICATIONS

Yemeni NGOs also release studies and reports necessary for their programs; human rights organizations monitor and document abuses in their field, and these materials are generally used in their advocacy campaigns. NGOs publish studies on restrictions on civil and political rights, and discrimination in the legal system, as well as reports on the general state of human rights, and media statements on specific violations. Women's organizations tend to focus on publishing legal studies, which track discrimination against women in the constitution and other legislation. These organizations also publish statistical and analytical reports about different forms of violence against in society, based on their monitoring and documentation. The Arab Sisters Forum for Human Rights implemented a three-year program to monitor and document violence against women and children, focusing mainly on rape. Based on this information, it released monthly and annual statistical and analytical reports on rape in Yemen. It also conducted an extended study under the same program, titled "protection is a right."

NGOs interested in childhood protection also engage in similar activities. SEYAJ Organization and the Democracy School publish monitoring reports about childhood and violations against children. Within their awareness campaigns, they also produce posters about various forms of violence against children, such as child marriage and child soldiers.

Most studies include specific recommendations in the organization's field of interest, such as proposals for alternative legislative measures, or recommendations to change existing policies.

NGOs in Yemen publish relatively few press releases about their work, and most of those they do publish are done so online. When press releases are printed, they are not distributed or sold to public, but disseminated within the organizations' activities. For example, the Human Rights Information and Training Center publishes a quarterly magazine called *Our Rights*. It includes studies, reports, and news about the Center, and printed and electronic copies are only distributed to those who work with the center.

Many organizations' agendas and activities have changed since 2011, particularly activities on pushing to amend legislation to be more in line with the International Bill of Human Rights. The political transformation in Yemen has included work to create a new constitution for the country, and a new legal system based on the constitution and National Dialogue Conference. Many organizations participated in the National Dialogue Conference, which had positive results, including proposed texts for future laws and the constitution. As a result, organizations' work is determined by how closely it reflects the proposed constitution the National Dialogue Conference agreed on (the constitution is currently being developed by a constitutional committee) as well as a proposed federal system for the country. Under this system, six regions will have their own independent parliaments and legislative systems; this was also determined by the National Dialogue Conference, and will be reflected in the new constitution. This will be a new and unprecedented situation for NGOs in Yemen, which are used to working in a centralized system, with one parliament and legislative system, which is less complicated than the one proposed. As a result, NGOs across different fields will be forced to change their agendas and work strategies. This will be a great challenge for many of them, as most of the main organizations are located and work in the capital of Sanaa, the center of government authority. This will change significantly when powers distributed across different regions will receive decision-making powers and significant independence from the capital.

GOVERNMENT CONTROL, AND RELATIONS BETWEEN NGOS AND POLITICAL PARTIES

While NGOs do not have an official relationship to political parties, there are deep, close ties between many organizations and some parties. These relationships are no great secret, as many organizations are managed by activists with positions in political parties. For example, prior to 2011, Dr. Mohammed Al-Mikhlafi was director of the Yemeni Observatory for Human Rights, one of the largest human rights organizations in Yemen, and also a member of the Political Office of the Yemeni Socialist Party. When Al-Mikhlafi was appointed as minister of legal affairs in the transitional government, which was formed after the 2011 revolution and the GCC Initiative, he resigned from his position as director of the observatory, and Dr. Abd El Kader Al Banaa—who is also active in the party—took charge of the organization. The Yemeni Observatory for Human Rights is clearly yet unofficially affiliated with the Socialist Party. Similarly, the National Organization for Defending Human Rights and Freedom (HOOD) is affiliated with the Yemeni Congregation for Reform (Al-Islah). HOOD is headed by Ahmed Mohamed Nagi Alawo, a former parliament member from Al-Islah and a prominent political leader within the party. SEYAJ Organization for Childhood Protection is also headed by an activist affiliated with the Al-Islah party, Ahmed Al-Qurashi, and the Prisoner Organization is headed by Abdulrahman Barman, an activist originally from HOOD, and affiliated with the Al-Islah party. The General People's Congress also has affiliated NGOs, but they are not as popular or active. The General People's Congress was the ruling party prior to 2011, and was thus less concerned with being a player in the field, as it monopolized the political arena, public sector jobs, most fundamental civil institutions, such as the General Union for Workers of Yemen, and the Women's Union of Yemen. While, legally speaking, these organizations are NGOs, they have long been treated as official entities, because they were completely under state control. The General People's Congress' interests changed after 2011, and certain organizations began to reveal that they had a close relationship with the party.

Aside from the main political parties and the organizations affiliated with them, new political actors who emerged since 2011 also appear willing to employ NGOs' activities to their advantage. The "Houthi" movement (Ansar Allah)[34] is one such group gaining power, and affiliated with them is the Yemeni Center for

Human Rights. The center is headed by Ismail Al-Motawakel, one of their main activists, who in addition to heading the center, is in charge of managing Ansar Allah's human rights division. The Yemen Center for Human Rights Studies, which operates in Aden in southern Yemen, is headed by journalist and political activist Mohamed Quassem Al-Noaman. This organization is close to the Cairo Conference,[35] a moderate faction within the Southern Movement.

Civil society work represents a field in which different powers in Yemen recruit people politically, hoping to use other actors' activities to benefit their own agenda. This is made easier by the fact that NGOs are not very independent or advanced.

The problem of organizations becoming "politicized" is due to the fact that political parties have clearly realized:

> that these institutions and associations will have a role to play, and can influence the public, and thus politics as well. Parties became interested in these institutions, which became a tool in conflict; each party sought to control organizations they have influence over.[36]

The state uses its intelligence apparatus to illegally monitor NGOs, especially human rights organizations, as they are seen as troublesome enemies for their work uncovering human rights violations in which the state is complicit.

The Law of Associations gives the Ministry of Social Affairs the right to legally monitor and supervise these organizations. Thus, implicitly, the ministry has the right to supervise these organizations' activities, financial resources, funding sources, and how resources are being handled. Article 19 of the law states that civil institutions and associations cannot conduct activities of a political nature, nor they can engage in any electoral campaigning or use any portion of their money for these purposes, whether directly or indirectly. The law also specifies a number of procedures and punishments for violators, the harshest of which leads to the NGO being dissolved. This implicitly puts NGOs under the sword of governmental supervision; the text of the law is vague, and can be easily construed by the ministry to shut down an organization entirely if any of its activities displease the ministry.

INTERNATIONAL PRESSURE, AND PARTNERSHIPS BETWEEN NGOS AND THE GOVERNMENT

In 2012 a donor conference on aid for Yemen was held in the Saudi capital of Riyadh. One of the most important elements of the meeting was international pressure on Yemen to actively commit itself to building sustainable partnership with civil society. As a result, an important document, the "Partnership Framework between the Government of Yemen and Civil Society Organizations," was created. The national reconciliation government approved the document on 18 September 2013,[37] after being officially submitted by the Ministry of Planning and International Cooperation, which drafted the document with technical assistance from the United Nations Development Programme.

The document contains several items, including the concept of partnership, definition of civil society organizations, importance of the partnership, principles of the partnership, objectives of the partnership, fields of the partnership, criteria for partnership, and institutional framework for the partnership. It also contains general references, including four main annexes: an action plan for implementing the partnership, a monitoring and evaluation plan for the partnership, a reference study of the partnership, and a legal study of the partnership.

The document identifies civil society as:

> non-governmental organizations established by citizens, pursuant to the constitution, the laws and legislation in force, with the purpose of contributing to the public good and expressing the concerns and values of a segment of community members on the basis of ethical, cultural, political, scientific, and religious or charity considerations without seeking to make a profit or achieve political power.[38]

The framework requires the establishment of a Supreme Council for Partnership between the government and civil society organizations, where the members of the Supreme Council will be appointed through elections, in accordance with predetermined professional standards. Forty percent of the members will represent the government, and sixty percent will represent civil society organizations, taking sector and regional representation into account.

Partnerships within the council's work must include various development areas, including youth empowerment; women, children, and motherhood issues; poverty alleviation projects; health and community development; water, the environment, and environmental protection; education and human development; political development; awareness-raising; human rights; vulnerable populations; humanitarian relief; aid for displaced people and refugees; strengthening elements of good governance; local development; and areas of security relevant to citizens, especially those related to human rights.

In January 2014, the minister of planning and international cooperation issued a ministerial decree to establish a technical preparatory committee to establish the Supreme Council. The preparatory committee is primarily composed of representatives from relevant ministries and civil society organizations, and its objective is to prepare the administrative regulations and structure of the Supreme Council for Partnership, with the support of the Executive Bureau for the Acceleration of Aid Absorption and Support for Policy Reforms. While the

Supreme Council for Partnership was expected to be officially announced in June 2014,[39] the committee is currently working on it, and as of the date this report was written, it still has not been announced. Yet there are growing fears that the government will assume tacit control over the council, through individuals from NGOs close to the government and political parties working with them, and that many new NGOs established after 2011 will be excluded from the council. The terms of partnership state that organizations must have at least two years of activities and deliverables, and that they must be licensed and governed, and specialized in one of partnership's fields, among other conditions.

The council's tasks will be determined by the Partnership Framework, and will include developing civil society organizations by providing technical and advisory support and organizing capacity-building efforts to strengthen new elements of governance; improving them to meet the needs of the partnership; proposing laws and regulations on civil society organizations' work, or amending them and developing them; and proposing new opportunities and fields for cooperation and partnership between parties, to expand social partnership into rural and remote areas.

REGIONAL RELATIONS

Many NGOs in Yemen engage in regional collaborations with similar organizations, though this often does not entail more than participating in regional conferences and seminars. There are a few organizations—particularly older ones—engaged in work programs or regional networks; these include the Arab Sisters Forum for Human Rights, which is a member in the SALMA Network against Violence against Women,[40] the Human Rights Information and Training Center, the Yemeni Observatory for Human Rights, and the Social Democratic Forum, which are members of the Arab NGO Network for Development.[41] More recently established NGOs have no clear regional collaborations, as they still operate only on a local level.

PROMINENT INTERNATIONAL DONORS

There are many international agencies that provide funding for most NGOs in Yemen. Most prominent among them are the Middle East Partnership Initiative (MEPI) at the US Department of State, as well as the National Endowment for Democracy (NED), the National Democratic Institute for International Affairs (NDI), the Foundation for the Future, the Dutch Embassy, the European Union (EU), the World Bank, the US Agency for International Development (USAID), the German Agency for International Cooperation (GIZ), the International Foundation for Electoral Systems (IFES), the Friedrich Ebert Foundation from Germany, CARE from France, and Oxfam from the United Kingdom, in addition to several United Nations agencies, such as the United Nations International Children's Emergency Fund (UNICEF), the United Nations Development Programme (UNDP), the United Nations High Commissioner for

Refugees (UNHCR), and the United Nations High Commissioner for Human Rights.

These organizations are the most prominent bodies that fund NGO activities and programs in Yemen. Terms of funding vary by organization, as the funding agreement is based on the suitability of the proposed projects for donors' agenda and interests, and is made on the condition that the NGO is officially licensed.

The Executive Bureau was created after the donor conference in Riyadh in 2012 to accelerate aid absorption and support for policy reforms. While it is officially affiliated with the Ministry for Planning and International Cooperation,[42] it is completely independent. Within the Executive Bureau, a unit for Community Partnership and Communication was established:

> tasked with highlighting Executive Bureau's role and activities and establishing fruitful relations with various governmental bodies, civil society, and donors. It is also assigned to coordinate with partners in order to reinforce and stimulate partnership between the civil society and the government as a pillar of the Mutual Accountability Framework (MAF).[43]

The Executive Bureau is intended to help NGOs create partnerships with the government and international donors. It plays the role of technical expert within the partnership framework between the government of Yemen and civil society, and supports the preparatory committee, which works on establishing of the Supreme Council for Partnership between the government and the civil society organizations in Yemen.[44]

International donors are the lifeblood of Yemeni organizations; NGOs cannot easily obtain funding other than through these donors, and this has a real impact on their agendas and priorities. This is likely due to:

> hostile propaganda directed against them by traditional conservative forces, in order to raise suspicions around them, especially regarding their relations with foreign funding sources and their management of resources. As a result, these organizations and institutions have failed to earn support from society, or funding for their activities from the private sector in Yemen.[45]

Despite many NGOs' close relationship with and complete dependence on international donors, Yemeni NGOs do not seem to have special relationships with specific foreign countries. Charities linked to Islamic Salafist ideology are a notable exception; they have unique relationships with similar organizations in other countries, particularly Kuwait. Al-Hikma Charity, which has a Salafist ideology, gets large amounts of funding from Salafist Kuwaiti organizations, for example. Kuwait's role in this relationship is unclear, even though a large portion of the fund transfers sent by Kuwaiti organizations go through the Kuwaiti Embassy in Sanaa.[46]

There are also close relationships between the Charitable Society for Social Welfare (which is close to the Muslim Brotherhood), Qatari charities, and other semi-governmental Qatari entities, such as the Qatari Red Crescent. This relationship became apparent during the 2011 revolution; the Charitable Society for Social Welfare (CSSW) was a channel that several Qatari agencies used to fund health needs caused by the uprising, including establishing field hospitals.[47] Moreover, many Qatari charities provide free services to Yemeni patients suffering from serious illnesses that require expensive treatment, but only if they apply through CSSW.

CONCLUSION

As a result of changes in the country after the Arab Spring, NGOs in Yemen have been confronted with numerous complications since 2011. Both old and new organizations were forced to adapt and respond to changes in civil society and their work environment, changes that generated new priorities, needs and challenges—most of which were beyond these NGOs' goals, experience and activities.

This vast transformation in the country impacted NGOs significantly. It went beyond their agendas, which changed, and affected organizations' entire environment. Political powers' unprecedented greed for civil society work became clear, and they worked to establish civil associations affiliated with them to increase their influence among organizations. This was an important tool for political powers, as they fought for the most influence over various spaces in Yemen that had opened up when the former regime crumbled.

NGOs' experience in Yemen has not been idyllic. They have faced various challenges and problems, but with a continuous presence over twenty years, from 1990 to 2011, they have played a key role in creating a critical mass that may help further their agendas, goals, activities, institutional and administrative structures, and transparency. While change has been slow, there have been positive developments, and society no longer regards NGOs with suspicion it had prior to the events of 2011. The Arab Spring changed everything in Yemen at a fundamental level, and brought many things back to a starting point; everything is up for reconsideration, from the form of the state to everything related. This was not the only factor, as there are other changes that influence the future of NGOs in Yemen, yet the significance of the events of 2011 on Yemeni NGOs cannot be overstated.

These changes have weighed heavily on NGOs in Yemen since 2011, and it is vital to explore the implications of the broader context on the NGOs themselves, to understand the new opportunities and challenges they are facing and how to move forward. By producing knowledge about changing realities for NGOs in Yemen after 2011, this report is a step in that direction.

ENDNOTES

[1] The results of the National Dialogue Conference, which were relayed to the committee drafting the current constitution in Yemen, also guarantees the right of citizens to organize themselves and set up associations, federations and unions representing them.

[2] Dr. Abdulbaqi Shamsan, *The Freedom to Create Organizations in Yemen*, study published by the Human Rights Information and Training Center, 2008, p.14. http://issuu.com/wadih909/docs/arabic/1

[3] Ibid, p.14.

[4] Granting a permit to establish / found associations, cooperative unions and civil institutions, the National Information Center, adapted. http://www.yemen-nic.info/guides/gov_guides/detail.php?ID=16893#1

[5] The ministry has not released any statistics on the number of registered organizations in 2014.

[6] Dr. Abdulbaqi Shamsan, *The Freedom to Create Organizations in Yemen*, p.23.

[7] Faysal AlSoufi. "Non-Government Organization in Yemen." *Al-Motamar.* 9 June 2003. http://www.almotamar.net/news/1817.htm

[8] Granting a permit to establish / found associations, cooperative unions and civil institutions, the National Information Center.

[9] The author of this report worked on this project for three years, until its conclusion.

[10] Officially, the timeframe for obtaining a permit for any organization or association is about thirty days after all necessary legal requirements are completed, according to the law. The Ministry of Social Affairs and Labor is entitled to refuse any application. If an application is rejected, applicants have the right to declare their organizations by power of law two months after they officially applied for the license. However, such a declaration does not grant the organization legal status, and the organization is usually asked for their permit when they collaborate with another association on any activity. The ministry usually takes a negative approach toward unwanted activists, whereby the decision to approve an application goes through an informal security screening process. It is assessed by Yemeni intelligence (the Political Security Organization and the National Security Bureau) who evaluate the applicants, the nature of their activities, and the identity of the founders; they are the ones who accept or deny the request, whereas the ministry's work is essentially a formality.

[11] Several activists and journalists interviewed discussed their thoughts on changes to the nature of organizations and "political" turnout, including: Abdulrashid Al-Faqih, Executive Director of Mwatana Organization for Human Rights; Sami Ghalib, Editor of *Al-Nida'a*, an independent newspaper, and Suha Bashrin, a feminist activist.

[12] About Us, Support Yemen. http://supportyemen.org/ar/%D9%85%D9%86-%D9%86%D8%AD%D9%86/

[13] The Beginning, Support Yemen, http://supportyemen.org/ar/%D9%85%D9%86-%D9%86%D8%AD%D9%86/

[14] Interview with Sara Jamal, Director of Production of Support Yemen, in Support Yemen's office in Sanaa, Yemen.

[15] Sara Jamal, personal interview.

[16] The Observatory aims to contribute to the advancement of human rights, and civil, political, economic, social and cultural development; spread awareness; encourage respect for and protection of human rights in accordance with international treaties and conventions, particularly international legitimacy of human rights by considering it an integral whole. Specifically, it aims to:
1. Defend legality, legitimacy, the constitution and the law.
2. Defend an independent judiciary and legal professionals.
3. Monitor the development of human rights, and human rights abuses, nationally and internationally.
4. Draw the public's attention and official attention to legislative and institutional gaps and shortcomings related to human rights.
5. Monitor violations of intellectual property rights, and defend these rights.
6. Help offer legal support for human rights and defending human rights, particularly collective rights and rights related to public interest in political, economic, social and cultural fields.
7. Spread awareness about the necessity of rule of law and the right to a fair trial.
http://www.yohr.org/?no=3710&ac=3&d_f=139&t=5&lang_in=Ar
[17] The National Organization for Defending Rights and Freedoms (HOOD). Our goals are:
    1. Defending victims of human rights violations.
    2. Heightening legal and human rights public awareness.
    3. Improving legal and legislative frameworks.
    4. Advancing the role of the civil society in advocating for issues of rights and freedoms.
http://www.hoodonline.org/2012-05-28-17-10-00.html#sthash.VfNB6soI.dpuf

[18] The Center's objectives:
1. Spreading the culture of human rights and educating citizens about their constitutional, legal and human rights.
2. Developing civil society and expanding its sphere of influence.
3. Developing and promoting human rights and democracy.
4. Spreading a culture of informed Islamic thought and combatting extremism and terrorism.
5. Supporting freedom of the press and freedom of opinion, expression and belief.
6. Respecting and promoting the role and contribution of Yemeni women to politics and public life, and affirming women's equality as a basic human right.
7. Attending to young people's issues, particularly those related to human rights education (in public education: in primary and secondary education and in universities) in order to create a new generation committed to the respect of human rights.
8. Attending to the issues of young men and women, caring for them, organizing educational and training courses, and helping them solve their problems.
9. Monitoring human rights violations, particularly those related to economic, social and cultural rights.
10. Supporting young people's empowerment in political and public life.
11. Supporting women's empowerment in political and public life.
12. Attending to sustainable development, the fight against corruption, and spreading a culture of fairness in society.
13. Supporting and strengthening the components of good governance, transparency and accountability.
14. Supporting children's rights.
http://ycfhrs.org/?page_id=87

[19] An independent, voluntary and politically objective women's NGO in Yemen working on human rights issues (women's rights in particular). The index of human rights in the Arab countries http://www.arabhumanrights.org/countries/organizations.aspx?cid=22

[20] The Women's Forum for Research and Training is an NGO working to promote women's rights and democratic rights through improving the work of civil society organizations, problem solving, creative thinking, learning how to cooperate, share skills, and communicate, and encouraging active participation of women in the media. http://www.arabhumanrights.org/countries/organizations.aspx?cid=22

[21] In addition to the Arab Sisters Forum for Human Rights, the Arab Institution for Human Rights, and the Women's Forum, well-known Yemeni feminist activists include Amal Basha, Suad Qudsi, and Rajaa Musobei.

[22] The National Dialogue Conference is a basic political mechanism endorsed by the GCC Initiative, which organized the transition of political power in Yemen after the popular uprising against Ali Abdullah Saleh. This conference was intended to include all parties in the political process in Yemen, including those who had previously been excluded, such as the Southern Movement, the Zaidi "Houthi" movement (Ansar Allah), as well as youth and women, in order to determine solutions to complex national problems, including shaping the state, form of governance, and the constitution.

[23] The main purpose of the Human Rights Information and Training Center is to spread awareness and promote understanding of human rights, provide informational and clerical services, and train human rights activists. The main work of the center, as a private, voluntary, and practical institution, includes:
1. Creating training courses and specialized workshops to spread awareness of human rights, thus helping NGOs play a positive and active role in the community.
2. Establishing a library that contains publications about human rights, and brochures and leaflets issued by local, regional, and international organizations, as a service for researchers and interested parties. The library should also archive newspapers and periodicals about human rights.
3. Holding politically-neutral seminars and meetings to raise awareness about human rights, and identify principles and international human rights conventions. It aims to do so in coordination with other bodies and organizations with common interests, on a basis of equality and political neutrality.
http://www.hritc.net/index.php?action=showSubSection&id=17
[24] The CDF aims to support civil and democratic efforts to help Yemeni society achieve democracy, a civil society, and social justice, by raising awareness about civil rights and democracy.
http://www.cdf-ye.org/AboutUS/AboutUS.aspx
[25] Objectives:-
1. Spreading the culture and awareness of human rights, and abiding by the principles set forth in the Convention on the Rights of the Child.
2. Raising awareness among different generations of the importance of a democratic civil society.
3. Strengthening patriotism, transparency and cooperative, voluntary work.
4. Creating communities that believe in their right to political action based on principles of democracy and acceptance of others.
http://www.dsyemen.org/about.php
[26] Objectives: -
1. Enabling children to have stability and security.
2. Protecting children from physical, mental, psychological or behavioral harm.
3. Supporting the efforts of child advocates, nationally and internationally.
4. Seeking to create a community that can protect children's rights and interests.
http://www.seyaj.org/DEFAULTFILE.ASPX?SUB_ID=523

[27]The Yemen Family Care Association (YFCA) has been serving Yemeni families since 1976. As a pioneer in promoting reproductive rights and health in Yemen, it excelled in service provision, education and advocacy. Its quality reproductive health services have been accessed over the years by men, women, youth and children in Sanaa and other governorates.. http://yfca-yc.org/content/1-%D9%85%D9%86-%D9%86%D8%AD%D9%86/1-%D8%B3%D8%A8%D8%B9%D9%87-%D9%88%D8%AB%D9%84%D8%A7%D8%AB%D9%88%D9%86-%D8%B9%D8%A7%D9%85%D8%A7%D9%8B-%D9%85%D9%86-%D8%A7%D9%84%D8%AE%D8%AF%D9%85%D8%A7%D8%AA-%D8%A7%D9%84%D8%B5%D8%AD%D9%8A%D9%87-%D8%B0%D8%A7%D8%AA-%D8%A7%D9%84%D8%AC%D9%88%D8%AF%D8%A9-%D8%A7%D9%84%D8%B9%D8%A7%D9%84%D9%8A%D8%A9

[28] This coalition of civil society organizations, "UMAM," included the following agencies: Journalists Without Borders, the Yemeni Observatory for Human Rights, the National Organization for Defending Rights and Freedoms (HOOD), the Social Democratic Forum, the Democracy School, the Arab Sisters Forum for Human Rights, the Yemeni Organization for Defending Rights and Freedoms, The Yemeni Teachers' Guild, the Students' Union of Yemen, the Faculty Union at the University of Sanaa, the Doctors and Pharmacists' Guild, the Political Development Forum, the Change Organization for Rights and Freedoms, the Women's Forum for Research and Training, the Women in Media Forum, the Educational Professions' Guild, the Motorcyclists' Guild, the Center for Journalistic Training and Freedom, the Committee for Resisting Normalization, the Construction Workers' Union, and other figures in society and parliament.
The coalition was governed by the coordinating body, which served for a term, and whose members were selected every six months by the parties of the coalition.
[29] The information has been taken from interviews with a number of coalition members, including Balqish Allahbi and Radia al-Mutawakkil.

[30] Our Mission, HOOD. http://www.hoodonline.org/2012-05-28-17-10-00.html
[31] About the Center, Human Rights Information and Training Center. http://www.hritc.net/index.php?action=showSubSection&id=17
[32] The Message, Yemeni Family Care Association, http://yfca-yc.org/content/1-%D9%85%D9%86-%D9%86%D8%AD%D9%86/2-%D8%A7%D9%84%D8%AE%D9%84%D9%81%D9%8A%D8%A9-%D8%A7%D9%84%D9%85%D8%A4%D8%B3%D8%B3%D9%8A%D8%A9
[33] The Democracy School. http://www.dsyemen.org/about.php
[34] The Houthis, or Ansar Allah, are a revivalist Zaidi Shia movement founded in Saada in the early 2000s by Hussein Badreddin al-Houthi, a politician and the son of a prominent Zaidi cleric, Badreddin al-Houthi. The movement has fought with the Yemeni military six times between 2003 and 2009. Hussein al-Houthi was killed in the first round of clashes, and his brother Abdulmalik al-Huthi, has been in charge since. The movement has controlled the province of Saada in northern Yemen since 2011, and extended its influence to a number of other provinces such as Amran, Hajjah, and Al-Jawf, where it engaged in armed conflicts to establish control over the tribes of those areas, Salafi groups, and militias affiliated with the Muslim Brotherhood.

[35] Ali Nasir Muhammad, former president of South Yemen, and Haidar Abu Bakr al-Attas, the first prime minister of Yemen, lead what is known as the Cairo Conference, a moderate faction of the peaceful Southern Movement. It demands a two-state federal solution, along the borders of the former two countries. There are two other, more extremist factions, led by the Southern President [sic] Ali Salem Al Beidh and southern politician Hassan Ba'oum, which call for the separation of North and South Yemen, and the restoration of the former country of South Yemen.

[36] Faisal AlSoufi, Yemeni NGOs http://www.almotamar.net/news/1817.htm

[37] Reconciliation Government Recognizes a Close Partnership with Civil Society, News Yemen, 18 September 2013. http://www.newsyemen.net/news1933.html

[38] Definition of Civil Society Organizations, Partnership Framework between the Government of Yemen and Civil Society Organizations, The Executive Bureau for the Acceleration of Aid Absorption & Support for Policy Reforms. http://www.ebyemen.org/ar/documents/%D8%A5%D9%82%D8%B1%D8%A7%D8%B1-%D9%88%D8%AB%D9%8A%D9%82%D8%A9-%D8%A7%D9%84%D8%B4%D8%B1%D8%A7%D9%83%D8%A9

[39] Partnership and Networking Unit, The Executive Bureau for the Acceleration of Aid Absorption & Support for Policy Reforms. http://www.ebyemen.org/ar/about/%D9%88%D8%AD%D8%AF%D8%A9%D8%A7%D9%84%D8%B4%D8%B1%D8%A7%D9%83%D8%A9-%D9%88%D8%A7%D9%84%D8%AA%D9%88%D8%A7%D8%B5%D9%84

[40] The Salma Project. http://www.amanjordan.org/salma/wmview.php?ArtID=1

[41] Members in the network, Arab NGO Network for Development. http://www.annd.org/arabic/members.php?page=Our%20Members

[42] The Executive Bureau for the Acceleration of Aid Absorption and Support for Policy Reforms was created by Presidential Decree No. 22 of 2013 as an independent body within the Ministry of Planning and International Cooperation, given the close connection between the Executive Bureau's work and the Ministry. The Executive Bureau was officially launched on 9 December 2013 in the presence of the Minister of Planning, Deputy Chair of the Board of Directors, donors, ministries and relevant government bodies. Overview. http://www.ebyemen.org/ar/about/%D8%B9%D9%86-%D8%A7%D9%84%D8%AC%D9%87%D8%A7%D8%B2%D8%A7%D9%84%D8%AA%D9%86%D9%81%D9%8A%D8%B0%D9%8A

[43] The Executive Bureau for the Acceleration of Aid Absorption & Support for Policy Reforms. http://www.ebyemen.org/ar/about/%D9%88%D8%AD%D8%AF%D8%A9%D8%A7%D9%84%D8%B4%D8%B1%D8%A7%D9%83%D8%A9-%D9%88%D8%A7%D9%84%D8%AA%D9%88%D8%A7%D8%B5%D9%84

[44] See reference above on the Partnership Framework, its objectives and what will might entail.

[45] Faisal AlSoufi, NGO's in Yemen, AlMotamar.net. http://www.almotamar.net/news/1817.htm

[46] Information from a source working at the Kuwaiti Embassy in Sanaa who prefers to remain unnamed.

[47] Press releases and the media spoke about Qatari financial support through charitable institutions affiliated with the Muslim Brotherhood, the most prominent is the Charitable Society for Social Welfare.

Palestinian Civil Society:
Study of Changes in Palestinian NGOs 2006 – 2014
Firas Jaber & Iyad Al Riyahi

INTRODUCTION

REVIEW OF IMPORTANT MOMENTS

The majority of studies and research conducted about Palestinian civil society recognize a unique trait of this organizational activity. This uniqueness is due to the development of this field through time, which went against the way civil societies developed in other countries and was even contrary to the theoretical concept of civil society itself. While most civil societies were established and developed within "a state," Palestinian civil society was established in the absence of a state, without national independence, and without sovereignty over the land.[1]

These different circumstances (which still exist) require that these NGOs operate according to revolutionary and emancipatory objectives and operating mechanisms, and for decades this was the agenda according to which these NGOs operated. Despite their work toward emancipation, these organizations are now required, especially after the Oslo accords, to play a role more suitable for NGOs operating in an independent and sovereign state. Many programs were funded based on this new role (most funds were spent on capacity building, good governance, and the adoption of laws, legislations and human rights treaties etc.). However, this financial support is not translated into political support for Palestinians in the hallways of the United Nations Human Rights Council, support for Palestine's accession to the ICC, breaking the siege on Gaza, or even stopping the building of the apartheid wall etc. The community of international donors only gives this financial support because it is concerned with ensuring the continuity of certain "functions" which can support the Palestinian society and always keep it just one step away from complete breakdown. This adds a new challenge to civil organizations in terms of their ability to maintain the balance between their national and social goals, and survival requirements due to their extreme reliance on external funding.

On the other hand, other studies have taken a completely different position. These studies considered that the ability of Palestinian civil society to develop is tied to its ability to move away from politics. According to the study conducted by Francesco and Athamne for the European Union delegation, there are many risks threatening the work of civil society organizations. For instance, the relationship between politics and these organizations is not clearly defined; new specific roles should be determined for these organizations so that they serve the transition to democracy and the current state-building in the Occupied Territories. It is not clear why those two authors considered this diagnosis appropriate to the Palestinian situation and to the role of civil society in Palestine, especially considering that building the state and democratic transition is in and of itself a problematic process, as the Palestinian Territories are under occupation. Civil organizations focusing on community-based democratic work and ignoring their political role end up being isolated from reality, which reinforces the prevailing criticism and impression of these organizations among many Palestinians. This is what Linda Tabar and Sari Hanafi pointed out in their book *The Emergence of a Palestinian Globalized Elite*; they claim that despite the emergence of these organizations within the Palestinian national movement and their subsequent involvement in development activities, they have been faced with enormous pressure to keep politics away from their work.[2]

It is important here to note the confusion regarding the designation of organizations. Civil society organizations are sometimes referred to as civil organizations and other times as NGOs. This study uses the term civil organizations to refer to the prevailing organizational action before the eighties and sometimes during the first intifada, when organizations were led through local community initiatives, endowments, or community, local and political action. The organizations were often affiliated with political parties and local political movements, even if they often also had international support. This study uses the term NGOs to refer to non-governmental work implemented through the support of non-local donors, whether or not they are foreign public authorities.

EXTERNAL FUNDING CRITICISM

Local NGOs never criticize their Western donors directly because they are afraid that the donors would cut their funding. This fear and the inability to influence donors are the result of the fact that there are more than ten competing organizations working in the same field of specialization. Competition has increased by 185 percent since 2006.[3] This kind of competition has made the local Palestinian NGOs incapable of influencing their donors. Ms. Zouheira Fares confirms this reality. She has been working with NGOs for the last two decades and she says that some institutions refuse to fund certain NGOs' programs for political and/or professional reasons and then agree to fund the same program executed by other NGOs operating in the same field or specialization.[4]

With time, Palestinians started to develop a negative attitude toward NGOs because of their proliferation and inefficiency in tackling daily life obstacles caused by the occupation. Mustafa al-Barghouthi indicated that after 1993, and upon the Oslo accords, many foreign associations and donors came to Palestine. This made it easier for NGOs to work in Palestine because it reduced contact with the Israeli occupation. These organizations chose to work directly in the country and not through Palestinian organizations, which weakened the Palestinian organizations' ability to control the donors' agendas.[5]

Although many NGOs criticize the Oslo accords and demand their termination, they are at the same time involved in various activities for which these accords have paved the way. After 2006, these NGOs became even more involved when they called for new elections for the Palestinian Legislative Council, and then got further involved in the discourse about "building the state" adopted when Salam Fayyad took over the responsibility of the caretaker government in 2007. Fayyad succeeded in attracting a number of NGOs directors in order to obtain "legitimacy" from civil society for his own plans and visions.

CIVIL SOCIETY ORGANIZATIONS AND THE ARAB SPRING

With the emergence of various shifts in Arab civil society following the revolutions in several Arab states, there was an increase in the number of NGOs in countries which were not used to having this form of social work, particularly in Libya and Syria. Other NGOs in Tunisia and Egypt expanded the scope of their work, and new organizations emerged as international organizations became more and more interested in working in these countries; they established new offices or increased their funding of programs addressing the issues of democracy, protection of women, and promotion of political engagement. By then, Palestinian NGOs had moved to another phase following the massive polarization caused by the Palestinian political division between Hamas and Fatah. As a result, NGOs in the West Bank are under the authority of Fatah while those in Gaza are under the authority of Hamas. It can be said that, since 2006, the trend has been the establishment of NGOs affiliated with political parties which have seen civil society as an opportunity to reclaim control over key positions in society, in other words, the left has monopolized civil work. Moreover, initiatives launched by individuals not affiliated with political parties to create this type of organizations have increased. This is yet another indicator of the increase in the number of professional NGOs at the expense of active organizations affiliated to political parties.

NON-GOVERNMENTAL ORGANIZATIONS TORN BETWEEN POLITICAL PARTIES AND DONORS' AGENDAS

Many players, including political parties and international donors, interact within the arena of civil society organizations and associations. In addition, there are often internal tensions between board members. The most important shift is the rising influence of donors, and the fading role of the old relief, charity, and voluntary framework among a good number of donors. Nowadays, organizations get funding if they are deemed "professional" by the majority of Western donors.

This was clearly noticeable in the shift that occurred in popular women's organizations. They were transformed from popular institutions with a national agenda, to human rights organizations working within the framework of preparation for the "state." After 2006, when Hamas took over the government, secular organizations dealt with Islamic women's organizations with a sense of superiority, and sometimes they were in real conflict with them. The most obvious instances of conflict were noticeable at the Ministry of Women's Affairs (MOWA).[6]

Hamas's victory was not only detrimental to the political system, but also to civil society organizations, which were subject to severe criticism, even from their donors, especially when their work was compared to that of Islamic associations. In addition, as a result of internal criticism within political parties who had authority over certain organizations, some of these parties considered that it was time to restructure their relationships with these organizations.[7]

After 2006, donors opted to support organizations affiliated to Fatah. The budgets of these organizations exceeded millions of dollars in their first few years because donors were afraid that Fatah would lose the West Bank. Donors felt then that it was necessary to strengthen the role of Fatah in civil society. As the dominance of the authority alone was not enough, another source of influence and power was needed: civil society. This explains why Fatah was late in starting to establish modern civil society organizations.

It should be noted that civil society organizations started to move away, structurally and ideologically, from their early eighties form. These changes were due to the rising internal contradictions they had witnessed: popular development vs. political mobilization, organizational hierarchy vs. professional staff and social participation, political money vs. funds granted to support society. Researcher Rima Hamami lists the manifestations of these contradictions as follows:

1. Demanding an independent and persistent role for non-governmental organizations and their engagement in building civil society.
2. The transformation of the popular movement into a society of NGOs.
3. The transformation of popular volunteer-based organizations into elitist organizations, politically and professionally autonomous.
4. The reliance of politically affiliated organizations on general assemblies full of independent members and hiring non-partisan staff.

Hamami attributes the main reason for this shift to political conditions imposed by donor countries which consisted of long term planning, complete transparency, activities related to education or the provision of services instead of political mobilization, and preference for projects with "measurable" results. The second reason is the ideological shift from radicalism to a discourse limited to development.[8]

In addition to the changes criticized by Hamami, the shift toward professionalism also created a phase of conflict within the organizations established by political parties. This internal conflict manifested itself with the search for independent staff or professional general assembly members, which was part of the legal conflict aiming to completely separate the organization from the political party. This is what happened with the Palestinian Medical Relief Society, Badil Center, and Panorama Center. However, some left-wing political parties were able to rectify the situation and avoid this division; they strengthened their cadres' membership in the general assembly of these organizations, particularly in higher management. Now it is rare to find a director that is not a member of the party.

This created an arena where fights for control would erupt within political parties, and in the future yield a cycle of interest and benefit exchange among certain circles in left-wing parties whose action revolves mainly around NGOs. It would also yield an exchange of roles in the NGOs' boards of directors. It is also notable that individual initiatives have recently created many organizations independently of Palestinian political parties. These initiatives rely solely on a group of individuals and some regulations to guide and regulate their activities.

As a result of the shock caused by the victory of Hamas in the legislative elections, people began to pose many difficult questions regarding the extent to which the work of NGOs was in harmony with the vision of political parties, and to what extent the work of these NGOs contributed to the growth of popular support of political parties and the implementation of their visions. General elections were not held as in 2006, but if municipal and local council elections are used as an indicator of a status quo, they indicate a worse situation for these parties, which lost major municipalities previously under their control, such as Ramallah and Bethlehem. Therefore, this indicates that the revisions made by left-wing political parties in their NGO work failed.

The left declared its refusal of the Oslo accords, but the NGOs affiliated to it benefited from the enormous financial support that came with these accords. These funds were used to pass the unequal resolution process, and set up the infrastructure required for its success.[9] It can be said that the issue of funding distanced many organizations from the parties they were affiliated with. Furthermore, active cadres of the parties became more involved in a different field revolving around development and human rights. This form of party established NGOs is no longer the only major power in Palestinian civil society as there are other, equally powerful, organizations in terms of funding and number of employees. These organizations openly express their independence from any political party or even any political matter, and commit to being "neutral."

METHODOLOGY

The report issued regarding this study was based on the data collected from the relevant department at the Palestinian MOI in Ramallah. The data includes information about more than 1520 civil organizations established between 2006 and 2014. The average number of associations given authorization during this period is 190 associations per year. The report focused on studying the case of forty-two organizations of which the majority were founded post-2006. The study determined a specific timeframe starting with 2006, which it considered a pivotal year marking the beginning of a period of radical changes within Palestinian civil organizations since the Oslo accords in 1993, in terms of their numbers and their relationships with local communities, international donors, and Palestinian political parties, who lost their absolute control over civil organizations.

This study used the analytical descriptive methodology and the following tools to collect information and data:

1. Using primary information sources by accessing the NGO registration data base at MOI.
2. Collecting qualitative and quantitative data through a questionnaire designed to answer the questions of this study.
3. Conducting in-depth interviews with civil society organizations concerned with the evolution of civil work.
4. Various reports and studies about civil work.

THE SAMPLE AND SELECTION MECHANISM

Based on the registration lists provided by MOI of organizations registered in the time period from 2006 to 2014, there were 1520 civil society organizations and associations as follows:

- Number of organizations registered in the West Bank and Gaza Strip: 1529
- Number of organizations registered in the West Bank: 1278 (83.5 percent) of the total
- Number of organizations registered in the Gaza Strip: 251 (16.5 percent) of the total

The research team selected forty-two organizations to conduct case studies according to the following criteria:

1. Selection of thirty-five organizations in the West Bank and seven organizations in the Gaza Strip based on the overall ratio of registered organizations.

2. The organizations of the West Bank were selected and distributed according to districts, sectors, year of registration.
3. The organizations of the Gaza Strip were selected and distributed according to districts, sectors, year of registration.

The sectors represented in the sample are:

- Human rights
- Youth and sports
- Development
- Healthcare
- Charities
- Culture, heritage, and tourism
- Media and press
- Training and education
- Economy

OBSTACLES AND CHALLENGES

It is difficult to access primary information sources pertaining to Palestinian NGOs. The research team faced difficulties in accessing the lists of NGOs registered at MOI. Several months were needed to finally be able to access them. Despite the cooperation of MOI and the relevant department within MOI, the NGOs database is not set up in a way that allows the extraction of information for analysis.

The Israeli offensive against the Gaza Strip delayed field research with civil society organizations. The research team had to wait until the end of the offensive. Due to the damage and destruction of a number of associations and organizations, they resorted to studying organizations that could provide the required information.

There was a high level of sensitivity about information related to NGOs, and some employees were unwilling to give the team all the information relevant to their organizations, specifically information about their connections, funding and numbers of employees. Despite this, the research team considers that the response rate of NGOs was satisfactory.

The last challenge faced by the research team pertains to the objective aspect of these organizations as many of those registered are not active. When initial contact was made with them, it turned out that they still have "registration certificates" and the phone number is usually one of the founders' house phone number.

ANALYTICAL FRAMEWORK ADOPTED FOR EXAMINED NGOS

Forty-two NGOs were selected and distributed according to the district, main sector of operation, and year of registration, specifically after 2006, so that the effects of both the political division and the youth movement which spread during 2011 on new forms of civil societies could be examined,.

The distribution of examined NGOs according to districts of the West Bank and Gaza Strip was as follows:

Bethlehem 9.5 percent; Ramallah 28.6 percent; Al Quds nineteen percent; Hebron 7.1 percent; Jericho 2.4 percent; Gaza 9.5 percent; Rafah 2.4 percent; the remaining districts (Khan Yunis, North Gaza, Jenin, Salfit, Tulkarm, Qalqilya) 2.4 percent each.

The percentage of organizations with which interviews were conducted and which were registered prior to 2006 amounted to 14.6 percent, while 85.4 percent of examined organizations registered within the period of 2006 to 2014. The percentage of organizations registered during 2007, the year subsequent to the political division, was 12.2 percent. The percentage of organizations registered in 2009 increased to 19.5 percent, and in 2012 it was 9.8 percent.

As for organizations actually operating prior to 2006, the official percentage of registration was 24.4 percent compared with 75.6 percent of organizations that became operational post-2006.

The distribution of organizations according to their main sector of operation is as follows:

DISTRIBUTION OF ORGANIZATIONS
ACCORDING TO MAIN SECTOR OF OPERATION

Sector	Percentage
Women rights	19%
Human rights	14.3%
Youth and sports	11.9%
Development	11.9%
Healthcare	14.3%
Environment and agriculture	--
Charities	11.9%
Culture, heritage and tourism	7.1%
Children	--
Media and press	2.4%
Studies and research	--
Training and education	2.4%
Economy	2.4%
Others	2.4%

Thirty-one percent of the examined organizations are classified as organizations having a second main sector of operation.

MEMBERS OF GOVERNING BODIES IN CIVIL SOCIETY ORGANIZATIONS

Civil work stems from volunteer work. It is mainly the result of a strategy adopted by left-wing parties, which consisted of forming organized committees for volunteer work. These committees later became civil society organizations. It was during the seventies that organized volunteer work started, as it came directly after the Palestinians woke up from the shock of being under occupation both on the individual and collective levels. A group of young Palestinians met at the headquarters of "al-Ghad Club," affiliated with the YWCA in Al Quds, and they agreed to implement an educational program for self-development and learning over two years: 1972 and 1973. The emergence o similar youth groups in the city of Ramallah in the West Bank helped spread this kind of activity. These youth groups adopted al-Bireh Municipality Library as their headquarters, and Birzeit University approved a volunteering work course as a requirement for graduating from the university. By 1976, youth "volunteer work committees" had spread to all regions of the West Bank and similar committees were also formed in the Gaza Strip.

During this phase, it became evident that human development was important, and that it was essential to make it part of the efforts made toward national liberation. It was also important to provide services to a society under occupation, a society subject to the occupation's abuses and attempts to thwart its development and progress.[10]

Volunteer work–considered the pillar of civil work–is now witnessing a different phase where civil work no longer operates based on a large group of volunteers. As we can see from the results of the study, the minimum number of general assembly members is seven members, which is the minimum number required for registration according to the Palestinian Law of Associations. The largest number of members amounted to 390 members in an organization, which operates based on the input of all its members. In other words, its mode of operation is similar to the way syndicates operate. The percentage of the organizations that have twenty-two general assembly members is 12.5 percent, while 12.5 percent of organizations have fifty members, ten percent have twenty-six members. The average number of general assembly members is 43.7 members.

The percentage of organizations that have male general assembly members is 88.1 percent, and 90.5 percent have female general assembly members. The reason behind this difference is that most women's organizations have no male membership. However, analysis of the arithmetic mean shows that the average number of male general assembly members is 26.2 compared to 14.8 for female membership.

The minimum number of board members should be seven members (usually elected by general assembly members). The percentage of organizations that have seven board members is 62.5 percent; five percent have eight board members; 27.5 percent have nine board members, and only five percent have eleven board members or more.

EMPLOYMENT WITHIN CIVIL SOCIETY

It was noted that 24.4 percent of the examined NGOs do not have paid employees. This means that in order to achieve their mission, they rely on volunteer work and they operate as charity associations, grass-root organizations or clubs working without financial remuneration.

The percentage of NGOs that have volunteers working for them is 92.7 percent, while only 7.3 percent do not have any volunteers. The highest percentage of the

NGOs (14.6 percent) have twenty volunteers, followed by 12.2 percent that have seven volunteers.

On the other hand, 75.7 percent have paid employees. This means that the majority of organizations rely on paid work to conduct their activities. The highest percentage of organizations (14.6 percent) have five paid employees, followed by 7.3 percent who have nine paid employees. Only one organization has sixty-two paid employees. In general, the arithmetic mean of the number of employees in civil society organizations is nine employees.

IMPORTANT CHANGES IN THE NUMBER OF PALESTINIAN CIVIL SOCIETY ORGANIZATIONS 1966 – 2014

Over the past forty-eight years, significant changes have taken place with regards to civil work in the West Bank and Gaza Strip. These years also witnessed an increasing interest by donors and ordinary people to search for new organizational structures beyond the family and political party. This resulted in a thirty-five-fold increase in the number of civil society organizations during this period.

In 1966[11], statistics included seventy-nine organizations and charity associations in different parts of the West Bank and Gaza Strip. Twenty years later, that number reached 2775, and the number of the civil associations registered in the West Bank according to the NGOs census issued by Mass Institute on May 2011 was 675 associations, 31.1 percent of which were registered after the establishment of the Palestinian Authority. In the Gaza Strip, the number of associations registered at the Ministry of Interior was 575 organizations, seventy-nine of which were registered prior to the establishment of the National Authority and 496 organizations were registered after the establishment of the Palestinian National Authority. Charity organizations constituted 40.4 percent of the total number of these organizations. Youth and sports organizations constituted 30.4 percent, cultural centers 10.2 percent, relief organizations 4.8 percent, development organizations 4.9 percent, research organizations 3.5 percent, training and rehabilitation organizations 2.8 percent, and human rights organizations 2.6 percent. According to the Ministry of Interior, the number of associations registered officially in 2014 reached 2775 societies in the West Bank, occupied Jerusalem and the Gaza Strip.[12]

Number of Palestinian Civil Society Organizations - Different Years

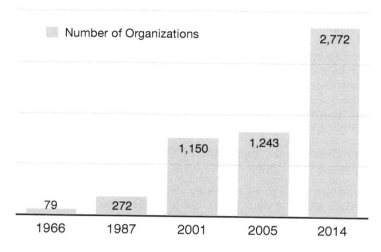

To date, the number of the organizations registered with the Ministry of Interior in the Gaza Strip is 901 organizations, 824 of which are local organizations, in addition to seventy-seven foreign, Arab, Islamic, European, and American organizations. The charity associations and civil society organizations in the Gaza Strip districts are as follows: 511 organizations are registered in Gaza district, 131 in the Northern district, ninety-eight in Khan Yunis district, ninety in the middle district and seventy-one in Rafah district.[13]

International organizations increased their presence and activities significantly in the Gaza Strip after 2007 as an alternative to direct cooperation with the government. Thus, significant support was provided to these organizations to bypass the need to deal with the Hamas government. Relief organizations became more interested in working in the Gaza strip as a result of the prevailing political and economic situation there, but the data does not determine the number of international organizations that started working post-2007. The table below lists the organizations that were included in the survey conducted by the Palestinian NGO Network–Gaza Branch:

Austrian Caritas	Catholic Relief	UNESCO Office
Japanese Cooperation	Handicap International	OCHA
French Cultural Center	War Child Holland	Save the Children
UNRWA	Medicines du Monde-France	The Japan International
UNRWA/UNDSS	Help Age International	Cooperation Agency (JICA)
ILO	UNICEF	The Friedrich-Ebert-Stiftung
WFP	UNDP	CARE International
UNHABITAT	Qatar Foundation	MSF
FAO	CHF International	World Vision
UNESCO	UNHCR	NDC
CMWU	Acted	World Bank
Qatari Red Crescent	FAO ACF (Action Against	SA-Rep. Office
Oxfam GB	Hunger)	WHO
Swedish Organization for	GVC UNFPA	Austrian Rep. Office
Individual Relief	Italian Cooperation	NPA
Islamic Relief	Merlin	ICRC
GIZ	Map UK-Medical Relief	Mercy Corps
Educed	UNIFEM	SDC
NRC	Al Ahli Arab Hospital	UNMAT
UNESCO Office in Gaza	ANERA	IMF
European Union	British Councils	Relief International
Middle East Council of	Right to Play	
Churches		

Most of these organizations working in the West Bank established coalitions and alliances. The most important alliance is known as the AIDA Alliance. This alliance regroups eighty international development agencies working in the Palestinian Occupied Territories. This coalition focuses on issuing reports regarding the economic and political situation in the Palestinian territories, and organizes related lobbying and advocacy campaigns.[15] Environmental organizations also formed alliances. These alliances are used as ways to coordinate between donors, whether on the official level or on the level of international NGOs.

NGOS AND THE ARAB SPRING

Of the examined organizations, 45.2 percent stated that, due to the Arab Spring and the Palestinian youth movement to end the division in 2011, more and more unregistered organizations were established such as youth groups, as this kind of organization does not go through complicated procedures. In addition, they do not need funding to work. However, according to a study on youth groups in Palestine emerging as a result of the Arab Spring, the examined organizations stated that the number of youth movements and groups which had emerged in Palestine as a result of the Arab Spring had weakened or disappeared, as is the case with the Independent Youth Movement and the March 15 Group. Their political activities had decreased and receded significantly compared to their beginnings. These groups rejected the institutionalization of their activities from the beginning.

The majority of the examined civil society organizations (sixty-nine percent) believe that Palestinian organizations were affected by the Arab Spring. On the other hand, thirty-one percent of Arab organizations deny that the Arab Spring had any influence on their programs and activities. In general, these organizations said that the Arab Spring affected them because funding was directed toward other countries, specifically those affected by this phenomenon (Tunisia, Egypt, Libya, and Syria). It can be said that the connection between youth groups and the Arab Spring is the clearest. The direct relationship (between the appearance of youth groups and the Arab Spring) is less clear for official registered youth organizations; however, the number of non-governmental organizations increased significantly in 2011 and 2012. According to data obtained from MOI, 371 new organizations registered during that period.

During an interview conducted with Muharram al-Barghouthi, the director of a Palestinian youth organization established twenty years ago, he noted that interest in the issues and demands from the youth increased among Palestinian NGOs after the Arab Spring. Moreover, youth organizations' work became much more efficient on youth issues. Currently, a democratic Palestinian youth network is forming, and the first issue it will tackle is the problem of the unemployment of a quarter of a million young Palestinians with university diplomas.[16]

POLITICALLY DRIVEN SECURITY CHECKS

It seems that in 2007 the role of Islamic associations was subject to strict security checks which restricted their activities under the pretext that they constituted the infrastructure for the Hamas movement. The same security checks were conducted by the security forces in Gaza on the associations affiliated with Fatah. According to Hamas sources and its websites, the Palestinian Authority in Ramallah closed more than one hundred centers and associations and confiscated their assets, as indicated in the table below.[17] The Hamas government shut down more than forty-two associations in the Gaza strip.[18] These statistics were reiterated by the websites of both sides of the divide (regardless of whether these statistics were accurate or exaggerated, the general conclusion to be drawn is that the security apparatuses of both sides dealt with the organizations affiliated or working with either side from a security perspective).

The majority (eighty-one percent) of the examined Palestinian civil organizations believe that the political division affected civil work in both the West bank and the Gaza Strip. A part of its impact is that the activities of these organizations are now limited to a single region; both sides of the divide closed the offices of these organizations, banned their activities, diverted their assets, and persecuted their board members. The table below indicates the number of organizations that were closed or put under control after the division of 2007. Usually, the Ministry of Interior (in Gaza or West Bank) shuts down these associations, and considering the political reasons for closing them, these actions have a negative impact on the judicial procedures, which are often difficult and pointless.

This table below shows the distribution of the associations affiliated with Hamas that the security apparatuses in the West Bank cities shutdown, damaged, or controlled after the division.

Organizations that were shut down:

City	Number
Nablus	21
Hebron	26
Ramallah	10
Tulkarm	13
Jenin	5
Salfit	7
Bethlehem	9
Qalqilya	5
Tubas	5
Jericho	1
Total	102

Regardless of the division, civil organizations allied themselves with the Palestinian Authority. According to Amira Salmi, in her book *The Development Illusion*, the NGOs always point out that coordination with various ministries is ongoing for all activities. They perceive that their role is to support the Palestinian Authority as the latter is unable to provide services on its own, leaving room to Hamas to compete with it. These organizations perceived themselves as competitors of the Islamic movements in terms of services provision.[19] Some activities not related to provision of services, specifically those aimed at influencing public and sectorial policies, required shedding light on issues on which the NGOs disagree with the authority, especially in the field of human rights. However, they did not cause any problems for the Palestinian Authority, thus it allowed the NGOs to carry on with such activities.[20] At times, joint training sessions were held, for example, the training of security services staff on human rights concepts, the joint efforts made toward implementing development plans, or the engagement of civil society in these plans, particularly, the last development plan of 2011- 2013.

The same discussion took place after the parliamentary elections and following the internal divisions which occurred either among the leftist parties or among organizations affiliated to those parties. Subsequently, civil organizations published studies and research papers supporting the possibility of launching a third stream (as an alternative to Fatah and Hamas). The Palestinian Center for Human Rights states the following regarding the consequences of the political division:

> The division that occurred in the Palestinian Authority in 2007 constituted another setback for human rights within the Palestinian authority, especially the right to create associations. Both sides of the divide in the West Bank and Gaza Strip made efforts to narrow the noose on the associations' activities, for political and ideological purposes created by the state of division. Both sides used legal means to cover these violations, by issuing regulations and amending laws, in an attempt to legitimize their actions against the creation of associations. The use of legal means for this purpose indicates a serious decline in the state of the Palestinian legal system and rule of law. In turn this indicates an even worse deterioration of liberties and rights of citizens.[21]

The violation here is not the prevention of the establishment of new associations, but rather it exists in limiting registration to specific political affiliations. As part of these restrictions on liberties, the relevant authorities resorted to imposing a series of new procedures for the establishment of any new organization. These procedures start with developing bylaws for the organization and unifying the form of these bylaws for all associations. Then a legal committee reviews the application request, and the General Intelligence apparatus and the Preventive Security Force conduct a security check (the aim of this check is to verify the political affiliation of the founders of the organization), in addition to a tax clearance certificate, criminal record check, and certificate of good conduct. Then the application is presented to another committee at MOI. In addition to all of these complications, local banks also have their own set of complications when opening accounts for these associations. These banks also coordinate with the monetary authority, which also conducts security banking procedures. However, despite the security element and the complications imposed on political rivals, especially those affiliated with Hamas, the number of registered organizations is enormous, and never before has civil society witnessed an increase as great as that in 2006.

GENERAL CHARACTERISTICS OF ORGANIZATIONS FOUNDED POST-2006

In almost all Palestinian cities there were newly registered associations and civil society organizations, but the majority of these organizations were registered in Ramallah (on average four hundred new organizations), followed by Bethlehem and Nablus. It can be said that forty-percent of 1529 organization are located in Ramallah, while in the Gaza Strip, the number of organizations registered post-2006 is 251 organizations, which constitutes 16.5 percent. The overall number of organizations registered in the West Bank is 1278 organizations of 1529, which is 83.5 percent of the total number of organizations registered during this period.

NGOs working in the West Bank and those working in Gaza are similar in a number of ways. First and foremost, they both have the same internal governance; both have a board of directors, general assemblies, and similar financial and administrative systems and similar programs, only the NGOs in Gaza focus more on relief work than on other development programs as a result of the siege and wars.

The table below presents the number of organizations established in different cities of the West Bank and Gaza Strip in the last eight years.

THE DISTRIBUTION OF ORGANIZATIONS REGISTERED BETWEEN 2006 AND 2014

	District	Number of Organizations
1	Jericho	32
2	Hebron	99
3	Al Quds	216
4	Bethlehem	131
5	Jenin	130
6	Ramallah & Bireh	400
7	Salfit	38
8	Tubas	22
9	Tulkarm	50
10	Qalqilya	32
11	Nablus	116
12	Gaza	149
13	Jabalia	15
14	Khan Yunis	54
15	Deir El Balah	12
16	Rafah	21
	MOI HQ	12
Total		1529

The most significant increase is in youth organizations (15.4 percent), women's organizations (12.9 percent), development organizations (11.5 percent), charities (11.5 percent) (these include associations named after the villages and towns of origin of displaced Palestinians are registered at MOI and are subject to the Law of Associations, such as Al Lidd Charity Association named after their hometown Al Lidd from which they fled, or Association of Kfaraana Families... etc). The percentage of cultural associations is 10.5 percent. These sectors constitute more than sixty-one percent of organizations registered in the West Bank and Gaza Strip in the last eight years.

THE DISTRIBUTION OF ORGANIZATIONS ACCORDING TO WEST BANK AND GAZA STRIP DISTRICTS FROM 2006 TO 2014

	Sector	Number of Organizations	Percentage
1	Women's organizations	197	12.9%
2	Human rights	98	6.4%
3	Youth & Sports	235	15.4%
4	Development	176	11.5%
5	Healthcare	133	8.7%
6	Environment & agriculture	95	6.2%
7	Charities	177	11.5%
8	Culture, heritage & tourism	159	10.5%
9	Children	74	4.8%
10	Media & press	31	2%
11	Studies & research	25	1.6%
12	Education & training	88	5.8%
13	Economy	41	2.7%
	Total	1529	100%

ONE HUNDRED AND NINETY-ONE NEW ORGANIZATIONS EVERY YEAR BETWEEN 2006 AND 2014

For forty years, the number of civil society organizations established and registered has increased significantly. This shows that more and more Palestinians are forming civil organizations and associations. One thousand, five hundred and twenty-nine new organizations were registered from 2006 to 2014, thus the total number of NGOs exceeded 2700 organizations. Regardless of the percentage of active organizations, the huge number of registrations shows the trend toward building groups or new forms of organizations that people can join.

NUMBER OF ORGANIZATIONS REGISTERED FOR EACH YEAR

Number	Year of registration	Number of Organizations
1	2006	194
2	2007	200
3	2008	205
4	2009	153
5	2010	184
6	2011	216
7	2012	155
8	2013	146
9	2014	76
	Total	1529

According to this data, 191 associations and organizations registered every year for the last eight years in the Occupied Palestinian Territories. An open debate and criticism has been launched about the role and funding of foreign NGOs, while other newly established local NGOs are still not part of this debate. The Palestinian Human Rights Organizations Council (PHROC) criticized the continuous funding and support of small foreign organizations which began to proliferate in the Palestinian territories. These organizations provide direct services, compete with the work of many civil organizations, and seize a large part of funding. This goes hand in hand with the continuous restraints imposed on Palestinian organizations. These restraints grow stronger as the internal Palestinian problems worsen resulting in the shutdown of tens of civil organizations, either through decisions using law as pretext or through direct takeovers.[22] This concern has been haunting Palestinian organizations for a long time. However, small foreign NGOs are not the only cause of this concern. What is being ignored is the kind of partnerships established between some local NGOs and other foreign ones which have no physical presence on the Palestinian territories. These foreign organizations take over a large portion of the funding as administrative expenses and consultant salaries while the actual implementation is made by the local NGO and its staff, or the funding is granted to a foreign NGO and refunded to a local NGO.

THE POLITICAL AFFILIATIONS OF CIVIL ORGANIZATIONS POST-2006

Surprisingly, seventy-one percent of the NGOs responded that they have a clearly defined and expressed national and political identity, while twenty-nine percent said that they do not have such identity.

THE POLITICAL AFFILIATION OF THE EXAMINED NGOS

Political affiliation	Percentage
Secular	22%
Leftist	41.5%
Islamic	4.9%
National (in the general sense)	31.7%

We noted from the table that the percentage and number of organizations qualifying themselves as leftist have increased. This is likely due to the fact that left-wing parties often rely on civil work when dealing with the social sphere, and at the same time the organizations that qualify themselves as Islamic are decreasing, probably because they are too afraid to express their affiliation or because many of them were shutdown, especially in the West Bank by the Palestinian Authority. This is confirmed by the fact that 53.7 percent of the organizations have responded by saying that there are different levels of relationships between political parties and the civil society organizations.

Seventy-one percent of the organizations do not have any work relationships or partnerships with Arab organizations, movements, or parties. This is the result of the Palestinian people's submission to the occupation and the restraints imposed on the people's freedom of movement and travel, in addition to the complications imposed on Palestinians entering some Arab countries due to security measures.

The new features of modern organizations have started to emerge post-2006, while in the past organizations with leftist and secular backgrounds dominated the scene. Today, organizations with religious backgrounds have emerged, or at least, the role played by charities affiliated to Hamas has now become subject to scrutiny. Also, the role that these associations play in strengthening the popular base of this political organization is under examination. On the other side, Fatah is satisfied with the authority and government bodies under its control and now seeks to strengthen its position through establishing NGOs affiliated to it.

Hamas' victory in the elections of January 2006 led to a boycott of the Hamas-led government by the West and to the imposition of an extremely tight siege on the Gaza Strip. This changed the forms of support provided by Western donors to the Palestinians: reducing development aid and increasing emergency aid to NGOs. All aid to non-governmental Islamic organizations and joint projects between Islamic and non-Islamic organizations was stopped.[23]

There are various political conditions on funding. The USAID "anti-terrorism" document is considered the most salient instance of political conditions imposed by donors on receiving organizations. We also noted that there are conditions related to political work itself and areas of activity, which limit projects to Area C, according to the Oslo accords.

Sixty-one percent of the examined NGOs stated that political and security conditions are imposed to the work of NGOs. The most salient and clear example of these conditions is the one imposed by USAID, which requires the NGO to sign the "anti-terrorism" document in order to receive funding.

Isam Arouri, director of The Jerusalem Legal Aid and Human Rights Center (JLAC), considers that the role of NGO Monitor[24] is increasingly strong as it expands its scope of action. Conditional funding is no longer limited to USAID, as now there is also Canadian, Australian, and Dutch conditional funding. The Dutch funding imposes non-written conditions. For instance, there are three or four cases in which the Dutch questioned Palestinian organizations who receive funding from them about what they did to anger NGO Monitor; they asked a few Palestinian NGOs about their stance regarding the boycott of Israel and pushed them to withdraw from BDS. The settlers lobby explicitly and directly demanded more pressure on Palestinian and international NGOs that support the survival of Palestinians in Area C and imposed new conditions. International organizations have started to accept these new conditions. Now, in order to be able to work in Area C, it is not enough to obtain prior authorization from the occupation administration; a military order has been issued stating that any goods transported to Area C need a transportation authorization; this order is clearly aimed at imposing more restraints on work in Area C.

According to the most recent World Bank reports, the restrictions imposed by the occupation authorities on the Palestinian economic regions inflict a cost of 3.4 billion dollars per annum. This sum would have been additional income for the Palestinians, had the restrictions imposed on the agriculture, construction, or water, been lifted.

However, according to official Palestinian statements, the Israeli Civil Authority continues to deliberately delay and obstruct water and other infrastructure projects planned for Area C. This prevents any development in these sectors and also undermines Palestinian efforts regarding future planning, including building the required national structure to support the future Palestinian state. Briefly, Israeli policies adopted for Area C permanently target the fragmentation of Palestinian lands to guarantee the expansion of settlements and exploitation on Palestinian natural resources.[25] Thus, Palestinian organizations face similar severe restrictions in this area, especially organizations working in sectors such as healthcare, agriculture, education, and infrastructures. Samah Darwish, the director of Grassroots, Policies & Advocacy Department at the Union of Agricultural Work Committees, shares her experience working in Area C and describes the restrictions imposed by the occupation authorities:

> The main obstacle is the lack of freedom of movement and access to some of the agricultural lands located behind the apartheid wall, in military zones, or natural reserves, in addition to the demolition of project constructions and land grabbing. Despite that many donors have recently aimed to work in this area, the majority of donors avoid working there. Moreover, the political positions of donors play a role in preventing funding for projects in Area C.[26]

NGOs OBJECTIVES AND PROGRAMS

The question regarding the shift in objectives, programs and actual civil work remains open and valid, as it reflects the situation of political bargaining Palestinian society is witnessing among its different components and with foreign parties including foreign NGOs, foreign government bodies, consulates and embassies, and even foreign advisory companies which started to implement "social" projects a few years ago, and make profits for their headquarters in foreign capitals.

The objectives of civil society organizations are diverse and wide in scope; they touch on almost anything, and for the purpose of identifying the most recurrent ones we grouped them into categories as follows:

1. Objectives related to communication, exchange of expertise, and networking on the Palestinian, Arab, and international levels, whether this communication, networking and exchange is political or cultural, or in the field of sports or rights etc.
2. Objectives related to democracy and participation, youth participation, women's participation, and sectorial participation through different tools and methods, including the media, seminars, workshops, empowerment etc.
3. Objectives related to the development of tools and methods of work with different groups, for example, academic tools, skills, capacity building, and empowerment.
4. Objectives related to raising awareness, be it political, economic, social, or cultural awareness, and reinforcing perceptions, which could relate to national or partisan causes and social demands.
5. Objectives related to the implementation of law, human international law, defending freedoms, and documenting violations by the occupation or the Palestinian Authority.

6. Objectives related to the provision of services and/or implementation of direct activities such as psychological, advisory, legal, and environmental services.

7. Objectives pertaining to defending the interests of a particular group or sector such as workers, traders, importers, and workers in agriculture, in addition to defending marginalized social groups.

8. Objectives related to relief/development whether sectorial or national. This includes operational projects, market skills, production or service provision projects, and development or criticism of policies.

CONCLUSION: A SHIFT IN CONTENTS AND WORK METHODOLOGIES

The 1980s witnessed the birth of several civil society organizations. Their discourse focused on development and resistance based on a resistant economy. This discourse was developed in two phases; the first phase was based on the idea that economy is a key aspect of resistance, while the second phase introduced the idea of building for the sake of liberation. The second phase discourse relied on two mottos: boycott and local production. The number of such organizations increased throughout the 1990s, and fierce competition over funding, the scope of influence, and fields of operation arose between those NGOs and the emerging Palestinian National Authority. In general, upon review of civil work discourse and action plans, we find that, despite the presence of discrepancies and disagreements, three types of discourse emerged from the work and programs of these organizations which have been involved in most of the work achieved by civil society in Palestinian territories occupied since 1967. These three types are the development discourse, the human rights discourse, and the services provision discourse.

The NGOs share a quite large amount of terminology such as "rationality," "free choice," "free competition," and "free market." Moreover, there are major similarities in the projects and programs implemented by these NGOs, for example, good governance, conflict resolution, women's rights, human rights and democracy, the supremacy of law, and monitoring of elections. However, the missing part consists of having a common vision for the development of the Palestinian community suffering from occupation on the one hand and overwhelmed by a neoliberal discourse, recently adopted and currently reinforced by the Palestinian Authority, on the other hand. This lack of common vision among NGOs in the field of development appears as an important factor contributing to the weakening of a key player within Palestinian society; it also limits contributions to the building of a national resistance program against "subordination which characterizes the relationship between Palestinian NGOs and international organizations and bodies, and reduces the ability of these Palestinian NGOs to respond to the 'needs or expectations of the local masses,' instead favoring the interests and priorities of donors." Western aid, particularly that originating from the United States, is provided to serve major strategic goals.

Consequently, since the agendas and goals of donors are clear, we consider that NGOs should clarify and sharpen their objectives and discourse so that they fit the Palestinian reality and serve to fight against the occupation and the neoliberal agenda.[27]

The conflict/shift takes the form of a continuous action within civil society among the secular and leftist elite on the one hand, and Islamic currents on the other. This can be understood in the context of defining civil society as a space where active groups battle each other, and alignments and alliances form based on an alliance with the authorities (Fatah or Hamas), an alliance with the foreign donors and their agendas, or the implementation of political parties agendas. Any civil organization can also operate within more than one alliance/conflict, or on the implementation of more than a one agenda.

The findings of the study clearly indicate that civil society organizations have become a conflict zone between existing local political forces, and with the international community, which is constantly trying to dominate through discourse and funding. Therefore, any increase in the number of existing civil society organizations, any shift in their action plans, or any introduction of new action plans focused on human rights, democratization, and good governance cannot be isolated from the context of the Palestinian cause and its future.

Civil society—viewed as a conflict zone between social and political groups seeking to expand their dominion over power/authority—is subject to constant foreign interference, and to the interference from the same political parties that use part of their energy, available resources and cadres to recruit grassroots tools capable of influencing the local community. However it seems that their motives are different. Instead of mobilizing and recruiting the local community to resist and fight the occupation, secondary matters tend to become main ones, and the agendas of political parties converge with those of international donors, who view competition and fragmentation as a major tool that allows them to dominate and control active groups.

Active groups in civil society can be divided into several categories, as some charities still operate based on the culture of helping and giving. Some grassroots organizations cannot fit Western concepts within their goals and programs, as they still envision themselves as part of the micro-society (the village, the refugee camp). We also find a larger type of organization that tries to combine national and developmental agendas and accept and deal with some concepts.

APPENDIX

STUDY QUESTIONNAIRE

Social and Economic Policies Observatory (Al Marsad) – Study of Palestinian NGOs
SECTION ONE: INFORMATION ABOUT THE ORGANIZATION

Name of Organization:

Year of Registration:

1. 2006
2. 2007
3. 2008
4. 2009
5. 2010
6. 2011
7. 2012
8. 2013
9. 2014

Actual Start Date:

Name of Research Subject:

Job Position:

Main Sector of Activity:

1. Women's Rights
2. Human Rights
3. Youth and Sports
4. Development
5. Healthcare
6. Environment and Agriculture
7. Charity Associations
8. Culture, Heritage, and Tourism
9. Children
10. Media
11. Studies and Research
12. Education and Training
13. Economics
14. Other/Specify

Number of General Assembly Members:

Number of Males:

Number of Females:

Number of Board Members:

Number of Paid Employees:

Number of Volunteers:

Section Two: Study questionnaire

1. In your opinion, what is the reason behind the increase of registered NGOs post-2006? Does this reflect a trend among political parties to establish their own civil organizations?

....
....
....

2. In your opinion, did Islamic organizations and associations work better on the grassroots level better than secular NGOs? Yes/No/ and how?

....
....
....

3. How were Palestinian NGOs affected by Arab revolutions? Was your organization interested in the changes occurring in neighboring countries? How did that reflect on your programs and events? Did you establish new partnerships with other organizations in those Arab countries? Did the donors' positions change due to these changes? (One effect is required, and the sub-questions are supposed to guide the respondent to talk about this effect)

....
....
....

4. Is there a trend to create unregistered organizations such as youth groups? Yes/No and why in your opinion?

....
....
....

5. Did the political division affect the work of NGOs in the West Bank and Gaza Strip? How?

....
....
....
.

6. The Human Rights Organizations Council recently discussed the presence of small foreign associations working directly with the community and considered them detrimental to civil action in terms of competition on funding with these organizations, in addition to their direct action in the Palestinian society. In your opinion is this a concrete phenomenon? How many foreign organizations have been created?

....
....
....

7. What was the conclusion reached by NGOs upon Hamas's victory in legislative elections?

....
....
....

8. Were NGOs subject to criticism because they were not capable of causing a real change by secularizing Palestinian society after the last elections?

....
....
....
.

9. Are there any political and security conditions imposed on NGOs? Which countries impose these conditions?

....
....
....
.

10. Does your organization express its national political position (Secular, Leftist, Islamic)? In your opinion are there still relationships between civil organizations and political parties?

....
....
....
.

11. According to your knowledge, do NGOs have work relationships and partnership with Arab organizations, movements, or political parties? Yes/No

12. Does the competent ministry monitor the activities of your organization? How?

....
....
....
.

13. Is there cooperation or competition between civil organizations working in the same district or sector? Yes/No?

14. Did the number of employees increase or decrease in the last three years? And why?

....
....
....

15. Does your organization have (Yes, No)?

   1. Bylaws
   2. Administrative system
   3. Financial system
   4. Document determining the organization's mission, vision, and objectives

16. What are the main objectives of you organization? Is there anything objective related to international law and humanitarian international law?

....
....
....

17. What are the main services/activities/programs of your organization (Name three)?

....
....
....

18. Were any amendments made to the services/programs adopted since 2011 (the youth action)? And why?

....
....
....

19. Do you have any long-term partnerships with a foreign organizations, consulate, or international development agency?

....
....
....

Suggestions and Comments

....
....
....

ENDNOTES

[1] Gian Costanini, Athamne Jamal and other, "Analytical survey of non-governmental organizations in the occupied Palestinian territories," 2013, http://eeas.europa.eu/delegations/westbank/documents/news/20110712_ngomapping_ar.pdf

[2] Sari Hanafi & Linda Tabar, "The Emergence of a Palestinian Globalized Elite: Donors, International Organizations and Local NGOs," The Palestinian Institute for the Study of Democracy, Ramallah: Muwatin, 2006.

[3] "Data study: Numbers and Names of NGOs established post-2006," The Palestinian Ministry of Interior, 2014.

[4] Zouheira Fares, interview conducted for this study, 2015.

[5] Mustafa al-Barghouthi, "The New Generation of Civil Organization's Compliance with Donors' Conditions." Interview published on al-Mubadara website: http://www.almubadara.org/new/details.php?id=1889, 2006.

[6] Islah Jad, "Islamic women's movements in the occupied territories (2)," 2014, http://palestine.assafir.com/Article.aspx?ArticleID=2823.

[7] Isam Arouri, research interview, Ramallah, end of August 2014.

[8] Taysir Muhaisen, "Political and volunteering organizations in the Palestinian context," Palestinian News & Info Agency, 2001, http://www.wafainfo.ps/atemplate.aspx?id=3981.

[9] Omran Al Rashq, "The Third Way in the Palestinian Context," The Center for Development Studies (CDS) at Birzeit University, June 2007, 68.

[10] Firas Jaber, "Volunteering in the Occupied Territories: Heritage used in political and institutionalized action," Badil, accessed 2/9/2014, http://www.badil.org/component/k2/item/1860-art6

[11] Abdallah al-Hourani, "Charity associations in the West Bank and Gaza Strip," Dar Al Karmel for Publishing and Distribution

[12] Wattan News Agency, "2775 officially registered associations at MOI," accessed 15/8/2014, http://www.wattan.tv/ar/video/93282.html

[13] MOI in Gaza website, http://www.moi.gov.ps/news/59890

[14] PNGO Network data–Gaza Branch 2015

[15] http://www.aidajerusalem.squarespace.com/reports-campaigns/

[16] Muharram al-Barghouthi, interview with conducted for this study, May 2015.

[17] Omamh, "Hope of releasing the associations upon the reconciliation agreement," accessed 1/8/2014, http://www.omamh.com/site/pages/details.aspx?itemid=21202.

[18] Al Hayat Al Jadida, "Hamas abducts more than 166 cadres of Fatah," accessed 5/8/2014, http://www.alhayat-j.com/details.php?opt=3&id=70529&cid=1781

[19] Amira Salmi, "Are NGOs a tool for development?" in *The Illusion of Development*, Bisan Center for Research & Development, Ramallah, 2010.

[20] Hassan Ladadwi et al., "The relationship between Palestinian NGOs, with the Palestinian National Authority and with donors," Palestine Economic Policy Research Institute (MAS), Ramallah, 2001

[21] Palestinian Center for Human Rights. The influence of the Palestinian authority division on the role of associations and their legal organization.

[22] Maan news agency, "PHROC demands the State of Palestine to join the ICC," accessed 2/7/2014, http://maannews.net/arb/ViewDetails.aspx?ID=568222

[23] Karin Gerster, "Palestinian NGOs and their socio-economic, social and political impact in the Palestinian society," Rosa Luxemburg Foundation, Ramallah, 2013.

[24] An "Israeli" right-wing organization which main activity is to incite donors against Palestinian NGOs (including human rights organizations) who have a national agenda, or against those against the occupation's policies.

[25] Interview with Shaddad al-Atayli, Head of Palestinian Water Authority in 2012, published on *al-Hayat* newspaper website: http://www.alhayat-j.com/newsite/details.php?opt=7&id=183731&cid=2707

[26] Interview conducted with Samah Darwish in 2015, especially for this Study.

[27] Firas Jaber, "Three discourses and missing vision," *Al-Akhbar*, accessed 2/9/2014, http://www.al-akhbar.com/node/27607.

Lightning Source UK Ltd.
Milton Keynes UK
UKHW021859160820
368343UK00008B/173